The Black Experience in America

THE BLACK EXPERIENCE in AMERICA

SELECTED ESSAYS

EDITED BY

James C. Curtis and Lewis L. Gould

UNIVERSITY OF TEXAS PRESS, AUSTIN & LONDON

Standard Book Number 292-70040-7
Library of Congress Catalog Card Number 73-111392
© 1970 by James C. Curtis and Lewis L. Gould
Manufactured in the United States of America

TO THE MEMORY OF **Martin Luther King, Jr.**

PREFACE

This collection of essays resulted from efforts at The University of Texas in Austin to institute a program of black studies. In the autumn of 1967, the Negro Association for Progress, forerunner of the current Afro-Americans for Black Liberation, circulated a petition asking for a course in Negro history. Thirteen hundred students signed the petition; the leaders of the NAP submitted their request to the Department of History; *The Daily Texan* and the Student Assembly endorsed this proposal.

The student petition coincided with the history department's discussion of the addition of a course on black history. Rejecting the suggestion that a member of the department create a new lecture course, the history faculty voted overwhelmingly to seek a prominent scholar in this field. The department realized that the search might extend over a long period of time; consequently, an *ad hoc* committee began to explore ways to sustain student interest while the recruiting effort proceeded.

In the spring of 1968, the committee suggested that the University hold a series of public lectures devoted to the Negro's role in American history. The University administration and academic community responded with enthusiasm. A grant from The University of Texas Excellence Fund provided the necessary monetary assistance. Ten outstanding students of the black past agreed to participate, and on October 14, 1968, Professor Louis Harlan inaugurated the series before a capacity audience of nearly six hundred. From then until the conclusion of the series on December 16, public interest remained strong.

Many of those who attended the lectures expressed a desire to see them in a more permanent form. The present volume attempts to satisfy these requests. Eight of the participants agreed to submit essays for this project. Six of the articles appear as originally presented, but Professors Harlan and August Meier have substituted other products of their research in black history. These essays, arranged in chronological order, indicate the scope of current scholarly interest in the history of American race relations.

We would like to thank The University of Texas administration, particularly Dean John R. Silber, for cooperation and support. Members of the history department were unsparing of their time and effort in making this series a reality. We owe special thanks to Professor David Van Tassel, head of the *ad hoc* committee, for his invaluable assistance in launching this undertaking. Professor Norman D. Brown graciously assisted with arrangements.

Austin, Texas   JAMES C. CURTIS
                                                            LEWIS L. GOULD

CONTENTS

The Black Experience in America

A Hidden Passage in the Slave Regime*

HENRY ALLEN BULLOCK

ONE OF THE MOST CONSISTENT ATTEMPTS to explain American Negro-white relations in historical perspective is the comparative approach introduced by Frank Tannenbaum[1] and extended by Stanley Elkins.[2] Relying upon contrasting social climates generated by two different types of slave regimes—slavery in the New World under the Spanish and Portuguese, and slavery in the American South under the English—historians of this young tradition have tended to project their findings to an explanation of the generalized

* This report is part of a larger study whose basic ideas were first presented in Henry Allen Bullock, *A History of Negro Education in the South* (Cambridge, Mass.: Harvard University Press, 1967).

[1] Frank Tannenbaum, *Slave and Citizen: The Negro in the Americas* (New York: Alfred A. Knopf, 1947).

[2] Stanley M. Elkins, *Slavery: A Problem in American Institutional and Intellectual Life* (Chicago: University of Chicago Press, 1959).

position of the Negro in the American social order today. "For many years," wrote Herbert S. Klein in his continuation of the comparative approach, "social scientists have recognized that the place of the Negro in contemporary American society was molded by the historical experience of chattel slavery."[3]

The emphasis that these scholars place upon the deterministic force of American Negro slavery not only overstates the case but also disregards the influence of subsequent experiences provided by the historical context. The position of the Negro in the American social order has not been static. Despite the social limitations he continues to experience, and to which he is now responding more belligerently than ever before, the Negro American has been experiencing a progressive trend toward a greater degree of personal emancipation. Instead of resting solely upon an anchorage provided by the roots of slavery—although strong roots were provided there —each stage of the emancipating process seems to have been supported by conditions inherent in the one preceding it. The comparative approach, therefore, appears incomplete as an explanation of the dynamic process leading to the Negro American's present social position. Another frame of reference is suggested within which his changing position can be explained. It concentrates upon certain elements of the social climate formed by the English slave system in the American South and identifies that system as the initial stage of a process of personal emancipation extending to the present day.

In its larger sense, the approach rests upon the concept of "historical accidents" and finds its evidence in a hidden passage to personal emancipation unintentionally provided for Negroes by collective responses to the nation's organized attempts to negate the Negro as a person. It is submitted here that there has existed in the United States, beginning with the institution of slavery, a denial of the Negro's selfhood and essential qualities as a human being, and an organized attempt to surround him with a social-cultural matrix

[3] Herbert S. Klein, *Slavery in the Americas: A Comparative Study of Virginia and Cuba* (Chicago: University of Chicago Press, 1967).

that would inhibit his personal development and blunt his creativity.[4] It was an attempt to create justifications for the limited opportunities that were given him in the first place; it was a process of negation that afforded a self-fulfilling prophecy. Nevertheless, the more these organized attempts achieved their goals, the greater the degree to which they contradicted the interests of those whom the organization was designed to serve. Responding to this contradiction, organizations have persistently found it necessary to devise new accommodations that continue to alter the normative structure of the larger society and thereby reduce the degree to which the Negro is negated as a person.

The path of historical continuity followed by this process has been meandering, but it has never been completely closed. Beginning during the slave period and within this institution's own social structure, it became less intense during the unstable period of the Civil War and Reconstruction. It even became blurred during the decades of institutionalized segregation, but burst forth in logic and personal aggression during the desegregation and separatist movements of the past three decades. Our concern here is with the first stage: how opportunities for the Negro's personal emancipation were accidently provided by the slave regime and became a platform upon which even greater opportunities could be erected.

The Rationality of the Slave System

The institution of slavery in the American South was planned as a rational order, based upon state mercantilism. A favorable balance of trade for England was to be effected through a functional marriage of agriculture in the colonies and manufacturing in the homeland. A monopoly of trade with the colonies was to be maintained, and a strong merchant marine was to constitute a bridge over which would pass raw materials from the colonies for manu-

[4] For a systematic development of this view, see Samuel Du Bois Cooke, "A Tragic Conception of Negro History," *Journal of Negro History*, 45 (October, 1960), 219–240.

facture in England and finished products for sale to consumers of the colonial hinterland. Out of the exchange was to come a greater profit to metropolitan England and persistent dependency for colonial America.

Indeed, though not suddenly, an agricultural economy to accommodate these rational aims did come in existence in the American colonial South. By the 1650's, a rather pretentious plantation order under the dominance of the nobility had centered in Virginia and slowly spread along the coast. The few colonists who had settled along the James River constituted a nucleus from which this type of economy spread northerly toward Maryland and southerly to the Cape Fear area of North Carolina and to the swamp country of Georgia. Many of these estates became fabulous show places that bedecked the coastal region of the South. The reminiscences of Dr. John Hampden Hill give us a picturesque illustration of these aspects of Southern life. "Once the Cape Fear was settled," he recalled, "there were many places whose elegance attracted wide attention."[5]

A more vigorous class was to set the rational economic order for the development of the institution of slavery. The pattern of class dominance began to change in revolutionary fashion near the close of the seventeenth century. The plantation economy took on a new form: requirements for a successful agricultural enterprise came to rest squarely upon large investments in land, equipment, and labor and the ability of an enterpriser to assume large credit commitments.[6] Those who were to share successfully in this revolutionary transition to capitalistic farming had first to wrest the land from the forest and the Indians. "It was a harsh and bloody task," wrote W. J. Cash.[7] It was a task unsuited to the aristocratic gentlemen and

[5] Unpublished manuscript of the John Hampden Hill Papers, 1883 (?), Southern Historical Collection, University of North Carolina Library.

[6] Elkins, *Slavery*, pp. 46–47.

[7] W. J. Cash, *The Mind of the South* (New York: Alfred A. Knopf, 1946), p. 6.

minor squires whose attempt to plant a noble aristocracy had been aborted.

Step by step a ruling planter class evolved to replace the aristocracy. The new breed were the frontier people who, by sheer pluck, luck, and scoundrelism became "a closed clique of property."[8] Bent upon profit, and taking any chance to get it, members of this class came to symbolize "the economic man" as prescribed by English classical economists. They, the upward mobile yeomanry, were to form the dominant element of the region's class structure. They determined the character of the region's economy, shaped its social norms, and enforced sanctions for deviations from the narrow range of tolerance they set for all the Southern people.

Several structural elements objectively indicate the rationality of the slave order that members of this dominant class instituted. The first was the large speculative investments of capital and the persistency of debt. As the slave trade developed, the economic destiny of this class became more and more dependent upon Negroes because of the large investment required for owning them. Individually, various members of the planter clique risked greater and greater proportions of their wealth in the interest of buying slaves. Items entered in their account books clearly reflect this. Concern with debt appeared as early as 1738, when the public had apparently begun to show some anxiety about reckless slave-buying. The South Carolina *Gazette* published a letter from a reader who was concerned about the cost incurred by the large importations of Negroes and feared that, in the end, it would prove "the Ruin of the Provence . . ."[9] James Baker, showing similar concern in 1764, wrote Duncan Rose, a fellow Virginia planter: "The African trade to Virginia must soon end. The people will not soon pay for Negroes they have already bout for observe, I don't call

[8] *Ibid.*, pp. 20–21.
[9] Wendell Holmes Stephenson, *Isaac Franklin: Slave Trader and Planter in the Old South* (Baton Rouge: Louisiana State University Press, 1938), p. 292.

those Negroes paid for when purchasers have a load of protested Bills to take up."[10]

Nevertheless, speculative investments continued into the nineteenth century. Showing signs of the pressure of debt, Charles Dabney, a Mississippi planter, after a visit to his son, William, wrote on June 5, 1830, that his unpleasant attitude while visiting him was because of worry over "vexatious imbarrishments in money matters" that had plagued him for the past twelve years. He advised his son to be more virtuous and industrious, to read the Bible, and, by all means, to keep out of debt.[11] The admonition was timely, for it came against the background of what appeared to be a mania of slave buying. For example, Jeremiah Watson of Concordia Parish, Louisiana, purchased twenty-four slaves on October 15, 1835, and in part payment executed a note for the amount of $14,704.91 at 10 percent annually. The note was secured by the slaves plus 650 acres of plantation land. The same note was sold the following year to John Gillespie of Adams County, Mississippi, for $20,565.21.[12] Guy M. Bryan of Austin County, Texas, wrote his brother, Moses, on October 26, 1857, that he would buy Negroes to the amount of $5,000 at any time, payable in twelve months. After selling his land in Bastrop, Texas, he became interested in buying more slaves through a Louisiana broker with whom he held a standing account. On November 12 of that year, he again advised his brother: "If you have a first rate chance to buy negroes when you get to Louisiana, do so. Contract to pay $8,000 or $9,000 down and the balance to the extent of $5,000 on time or even a larger amount."[13]

Even deeper economic involvements developed among slave-

---

[10] *Ibid.*, p. 148.

[11] Charles W. Dabney Papers, 1830–1831, Southern Historical Collection, University of North Carolina Library.

[12] Stephenson, *Isaac Franklin*, p. 64.

[13] Letters of Guy M. Bryan to Moses A. Bryan, 1830–1859, The University of Texas Archives.

owners themselves. Many became heavily indebted to each other. Illustrating how clearly members of this class separated business from friendship, Francis Terry Leak of Mississippi made the following entry in his diary: "Wrote James W. Crawford at the same time informing him that I was about to take possession of his land in pursuance of the contract between us . . . and inviting him to spend the winter at my house."[14]

These sales and debts indicate how greatly the wealth of the South had come to rest upon the productivity of Negroes. By 1790, the total amount invested in slaves had reached $104,639,000 as based upon the estimate of an average value of $150 for each. Over 93 percent of this total amount constituted investments made by owners of the Southern states and the Southwest Territory.[15] If the prices in the Charleston district were representative, it can be reasonably deduced that the total Southern investment in slaves reached more than one billion dollars.

The second structural element of the rationality of the slave regime was made necessary by the first. It was the development of a normative structure within the society that would reinforce the position of dominance the planter class had achieved. In order to ensure the continued existence of the system, the slaves had to be negated as persons; the property interests of the planter class had to be protected; the labor had to be efficiently organized; and the full protection of the lives of the planters as well as those of the white community had to be assured. Every slave code created in the South emphasized the theme of negation. Strict and certain discipline was prescribed to assure the unconditional submissiveness of all slaves. The brand of inferiority was burned into their consciousness. Methods of punishment were structured so as to awe the slaves and to give each a sense of his master's power, and relationships be-

[14] Diary and Other Records of Francis Terry Leake, 1841–1862, 5 vols., Southern Historical Collection, University of North Carolina Library.

[15] U.S. Bureau of Census, *A Century of Population Growth, 1790–1900* (Washington, D.C.: U.S. Government Printing Office, 1909), p. 141.

tween slave and master were so arranged as to elicit from the former complete identification with and dependency upon the latter.[16]

Standing between the authority of the planter class and the slaves were not only the Slave Codes and the judicial system through which they were enforced, but also an efficient patrol system composed of the poorer elements who gained their identity with planters through authority to maintain surveillance over slave property.

Pushed by the need to gain profitable return on large investments and reinforced by the sanctions behind the Slave Codes, planters carried the rationality of their economy into the organization of their labor. All economic roles and functions were clearly defined and "appropriately" assigned. Through an elaborate hierarchical structure of overseer, driver, field gangs, breeding women, and children's chore gangs, labor was skillfully coordinated to achieve maximum production. Its rhythm and tempo became attuned to the seasons of the year, the inclemency of the weather, and the nature of the harvest. The organization reflected the economic man at work in a plantation economy of capitalistic design.

Internal Conflicts of the Rational Order

At points the rational order sagged under the weight of its own rationality, and the voice that negated the slave as a person was somewhat muted. This occurred because profitable labor had to be preserved in its physical form and trained for increased labor value. Sick and ignorant slaves were more often liabilities than assets.

All historians who have researched the account books and papers of some of the South's most influential planters agree that the planter's cardinal principle of management was the protection of

[16] Kenneth Stampp, *The Peculiar Institution* (New York: Alfred A. Knopf, 1956), p. 42.

his slaves.[17] Remedies for particular slave ailments were carefully gleaned from almanacs and other printed sources. Sizable expenditures for patent medicines and doctors' visits upon the slaves were painstakingly recorded. Some well-run plantations had their own hospitals.[18] Guy M. Bryan's messages to his overseer, sent again through his brother, Moses, carry exemplary instructions concerning the cleanliness of the slaves and the personal care that should be offered them as a safeguard against poor health.[19] William Massie not only counted his slave population each year but also noted the incidence of morbidity and mortality occurring among them. Francis Terry Leak made the following entry in his diary on October 16, 1852: "For a cheap method of rendering domestic waterproof, and thus providing effectual means of protecting negroes from the morning dews in cotton-picking season, see receipt copied into my Scrap Book from the *Appeal* of Octo. 12, 1852." Expressing even greater concern, he wrote on February 5, 1853, "There has been great mortality among my little negroes during the last nine months." He followed this note with a citation of each case and its apparent diagnosis.[20]

Of course the planter had similar anxieties about his prized animals. When related to certain slaves, interest in the physical body formed a leverage for interest in the personality. At first the waning of rationality under the pressure of rising emotionality was faint. Feelings of economic insecurity and emotional bereavement at the loss of a slave by death became so mixed that one can hardly be distinguished from the other. Such ambivalence is hinted in Mary Austin Holley's letter to her daughter on December 23, 1832, relating to the loss of certain valuable slaves: "Hardly was this

---

[17] Ulrich B. Phillips, *American Negro Slavery* (New York: Appleton-Century-Crofts, 1940), pp. 261–290.

[18] William D. Postell, *The Health of the Slaves on Southern Plantations* (Baton Rouge: Louisiana State University Press, 1951).

[19] Guy M. Bryan to Moses A. Bryan, June 17, 1853.

[20] Diary and OtherRecords of Francis Terry Leake, 1841–1862.

[epidemic] over when the cholera came back upon us with re-
doubled fury. It was in the house this time and took one of the best
servants of the family. . . . You cannot think how gloomy it seemed,
their places so suddenly vacant."[21]

The diary of Thomas E. Blackshear reflects a similar mixture of
economic and emotional interests growing out of the loss of a slave.
He wrote on July 12, 1861, "My boy, Edmund, very sick; I fear
past hope of recovery." On the following day, he added, "My good
man, Edmund died. He was an honest, truthful servant and I shall
miss his service and influence a great deal." And on Sunday, July
14, Blackshear put the final touch to his expression of bereavement
by writing, "Buried Edmund with a sad heart. Gathered 200 water-
melons."[22]

Of course these were only faint signs that the crust of rationality
was beginning to crack and that the tendency for the system to
negate the slave as a person was losing some of its uniformity. As
social distance between the master class and some slaves decreased,
rationality waned and violations of many requirements of the Slave
Codes became more frequent. Members of the two classes became
more similar in their personal aspirations and personality structures. The hidden passage to cultural assimilation began to open
more widely for a few slaves.

Here again, however, the process was slow and the change subtle.
Probably the first opportunity for the slaves' assimilation of the
technical aspect of Southern plantation culture came through
their training in the manual arts. As the power of individual planters expanded, many plantation units tended to become self-sustaining worlds. The food consumed, clothing worn, tools used, and
houses inhabited by the plantation's people were all produced by
slave labor. A higher value was placed upon those slaves who were
trained for effective participation in this kind of economic system.

[21] Mary Austin Holley Letters, 1808–1846, The University of Texas Archives.
[22] Thomas E. Blackshear Diary and Memorandum Book, 1847–1865, The
University of Texas Archives.

A. T. Walker of North Carolina and Alabama bought his slave, Burell, for $887.50 in 1854 but sold him as a well-trained artisan for $1,150 the following year. At the same time, he bought Patrick for $1,000 and sold him for $1,130. Rachel was purchased for $725 and sold for $850. The profit on Walker's sales, after using the slaves for one year, was over 25 percent less cost of upkeep.[23]

Three basic passages to training in the manual arts became available to a select group of slaves, and each passage represented a step toward greater emotional considerations on the part of the master class. One of these grew logically out of the essentiality of training slaves in plantation technology. In response to this necessity, many planters developed an apprenticeship system for their talented slaves who showed high capability of self-direction.[24] Henry Harris of Clarksdale, Mississippi, was sent by his master to an iron foundry in Tuscaloosa, Alabama, where he learned to mold iron. The slave, Gregory, reared in Charleston, was observed by his master to have a love for tools. He was apprenticed to a master carpenter who taught him the use of the hammer and saw.[25] Frederick L. Olmsted recorded cases like these during his travels in the seaboard states. One slave whom he encountered, called "The Watchman" by his master, was entrusted with the keys to all store provisions of the plantation. He weighed and measured out all rations issued to slaves and livestock; he supervised the operation of all machines; and he made and repaired all machinery, including the steam engine. These skills were acquired when his master took him to a steam-engine builder and paid $500 to have him trained as a machinist.[26]

---

[23] A. T. Walker Account Book, 1851–1861, Southern Historical Collection, University of North Carolina Library.

[24] Ulrich B. Phillips, "The Slave Labor Problem in the Charleston District," *Political Science Quarterly*, 22 (1907), 419.

[25] Orland K. Armstrong, *Old Massa's People* (Indianapolis: The Bobbs-Merrill Company, 1951), p. 96.

[26] Frederic L. Olmsted, *Journey in the Seaboard States, 1853–1854* (New York: G. P. Putnam's Sons, 1904), pp. 54–55.

In numerous instances owners sought to develop the talents of their slaves within the framework of the usual work routine. Field hands cut logs during particular seasons, but other slaves, especially those trained for such purposes, built the plantation houses. Isaac Croom of Alabama used his slaves not only in the production of crops but also in the construction of all quarters. His magnificent home, Magnolia Grove, was evidence of their building skills.[27] Each November, C. W. Tait of Texas had his female slaves "sharpen their skills by spinning threads at night to make pillow lines." This art was not a common one. Some of the slave women who were trained this way became accomplished weavers; one belonging to John B. Walker wove 420 yards of cloth. Thomas Blackshear provided for his slaves to learn carpentry through a woodshop in which he kept particular ones busy at work. Handy and Richmond became two of his most capable carpenters.

The Waldeck and other plantations of Texas kept a seamstress and several assistants busily at work in sewing rooms, cutting and making garments under the supervision of the mistress or the wife of the overseer. The Jared Groce slaves wove the goods to clothe themselves.[28] Bell Kearney, speaking of the manner in which her mother supervised the work of slaves on their plantation, gave the following account: "Every woman sewed, often making her own dresses. The clothing of all slaves on the plantation were cut and made by negro seamstresses under her [her mother's] direct supervision, even the heavy coats of the men."[29] In order to be sure that the economy of slave training was maintained, Iveson Brookes of North Carolina included in his agreement with his overseer, Jan-

[27] *Birmingham News*, May 8, 1847, as quoted in James B. Sellers, *Slavery in Alabama* (Tuscaloosa: University of Alabama Press, 1950), p. 27.

[28] Abigail Curlee, "A History of Slave Plantations," *Southwestern Historical Quarterly*, 26 (July, 1922–April, 1923), 261.

[29] Belle Kearney, *A Slaveholder's Daughter* (New York: The Abbey Press, 1900), p. 3.

uary 1, 1849, that he was to manage the slaves and make the women of each place spin and weave clothing for all the workers.[30]

The economic motivations behind these opportunities were well served. Southern planters were able to grow their own supply of skilled labor this way. Although most of them thought the Negro's place was in the fields, many masters had long felt justified in turning capable Negroes into carpenters, masons, cobblers, and weavers. A few advocated and practiced the use of slaves as factory workers.[31] This kind of training made slave labor much more flexible than did the strict field-hand system.

Other opportunities for developing certain kinds of special skills must have come to the slaves through the provisions of wills made by their owners. As early as 1769, Margaret Page of Georgia provided in her will that her mulatto slave, Peter, should be educated and taught a beneficial trade until he was twenty-one, after which he should be freed.[32] Nathan Harris of Alabama stipulated particularly in his will that three Negro children—Margaret, Mary, and Thomas—be respectively taught sewing, dressmaking, and some mechanical trade for a term of five years.[33]

As a pool of skilled labor developed within the slave population, additional opportunities for the emancipation of the person were created. There emerged the system of hiring out slaves to varied kinds of employers. In this system, the owner kept title to the slave, but the employer purchased title to the slave's labor. The purchaser was expected to use the slave for a definite purpose, over a definite period of time, and at a stipulated price.

[30] Iveson Lewis Brookes Papers, 1793–1865, Southern Historical Collection, University of North Carolina Library.

[31] Avery O. Craven, *The Growth of Southern Nationalism, 1848–1861* (Baton Rouge: Louisiana State University Press, 1953), p. 249.

[32] John P. Corry, "Education in Colonial Georgia," *Georgia Historical Quarterly*, 16 (June, 1923), 141.

[33] Sellers, *Slavery in Alabama*, p. 121.

Here, again, the educational value of this policy was purely incidental and not the result of direct purpose. Of the many motivations that inspired the pattern, not one had education of the slaves as its goal. At times the policy sprang from sheer class consciousness, growing out of a desire to maintain status in the slaveholding clique or a psychology of being too proud to work. As the institution of slavery grew, it became somewhat fashionable in Southern society to own slaves, since ownership was considered a status symbol of the new aristocracy. Consequently, many owners purchased Negroes first and found something for them to do later. Hiring-out, therefore, was a convenient means of enjoying the "luxury" of slave ownership. Through their social influence and political power, owners found it very easy to get jobs for their "hands"; they could offer employers very accommodating terms.[34] Once certain types of jobs became identified with slave labor, white labor tended to shun them, feeling the work to be humiliating. This type of pride naturally created a labor vacuum into which hired slaves were freely poured.

Other motives for hiring-out originated in special circumstances. Executors, burdened with their own responsibilities, found it difficult to work slaves under their supervision. Therefore, hiring them to an employer for the benefit of orphans and other youthful heirs was a practical method of assuring the slaves' upkeep. At times, the services of slaves were offered in payment of debts. Ralph D. Flanders cites the case of Farish Carter of Georgia who, in 1828, received a letter from one of his debtors saying, "I have this day purchased a likely negro man. He is about 18 years old. I wish you to take him and let him work out what I am owing you if you will have him . . . I must get out of debt without having to sell my negroes which would ruin me."[35]

[34] Bernard Mandell, *Labor, Free and Slave* (New York: Associated Authors, 1955), p. 35.

[35] Ralph D. Flanders, *Plantation Slavery in Georgia* (Chapel Hill: The University of North Carolina Press, 1933), p. 194.

Most of all, however, slave hiring was due directly to the profit motive. Well-trained slaves hired at very good prices, and few owners holding them failed to take advantage of their value. Although the physical condition, age, sex, and disposition of the slave influenced his value, his industrial training proved an important factor in determining the wage an owner was paid for his services. Negro carpenters, coopers, blacksmiths, cooks, and shoemakers brought especially high prices. Of course these prices were a logical function of the cost of keeping a slave as compared with the cost of free labor. Long after mechanics, coachmen, cooks, and most skilled servants were too old for the slave market, they could be hired out for more than double a good interest and what they could bring at sale.[36] Therefore, many of the slaves who worked in the cities and towns of the South were hired from planters of neighboring plantations.

Hiring-out offered some degree of self-emancipation to Negro slaves. The slave who was so used very readily gained an awareness that he was the supporter of the family who owned him. Although some of these slaves could pick their own employers, they were kept in close touch with their masters, and this touch was often one of great personal concern and individual freedom. In speaking of her father's policy in this regard, Susan Smedes reported that he refused to hire out his young blacksmith for $600 per year because he did not want him to work hard enough to be worth that amount to his employer.[37] Individual members of the planter class felt that the system allowed too much freedom for the slave, and hiring-out was eventually forbidden in every state.[38]

[36] Frederic Bancroft, *Slave Trading in the Old South* (Baltimore: J. H. Furst Company, 1931), pp. 145–146.
[37] Susan D. Smedes, *A Southern Planter* (London: John Murray, 1889), p. 61.
[38] For examples of laws prohibiting masters from allowing slaves to hire their own time, see V. Alton Moody, "Slavery on Louisiana Sugar Plantations," *Louisiana Historical Quarterly*, 1 (April, 1924), 112; *Digest of the Penal Laws*

Nevertheless, it was freely practiced with extremely rare instances of prosecution.

An even greater indication of the emancipating force of this policy was the number of blacks, slave and free, who were employed at various skilled occupations in 1848. Using the industrial census of Charleston, Ulrich B. Phillips showed how widely Negroes were dispersed over the various occupational classes of that South Carolina city. Of fifty occupations listed, free Negroes were employed in all but eight and slaves were employed in all but thirteen. Although they concentrated in domestic service, Negroes fairly well controlled such occupations as carpenters, masons and stone cutters, blacksmiths, ship carpenters and joiners, barbers and hair dressers, and bakers. Slaves represented 47 to 67 percent of all employed in these occupations.[39] Despite white opposition, the practice of training slaves in the manual arts continued to make the plantation, at least in part, what Booker T. Washington called an "industrial school."[40]

Indulgence of Slaves and the Invasion of
the Rational Order by Emotional Needs

It was not long before the rational character of the slave system became somewhat infected by the emotional needs that this rationality tended to generate within the planter class. As social distance between this class and a few favored slaves lessened, a greater degree of intimacy of association developed, and the slaves gained more emancipated conceptions of themselves. These contacts

---

of the State of Louisiana (New Orleans, 1841); and Oliver H. Prince, A Digest of the Laws of the State of Georgia (Athens, 1837).

[39] Ulrich B. Phillips, "The Slave Labor in the Charleston District," *Political Science Quarterly*, 22 (1907), 434–435.

[40] Booker T. Washington, "Industrial Education for the Negro," in W. E. B. Du Bois, *The Negro Problem* (New York: James Pott and Company, 1903), p. 11, and Booker T. Washington and W. E. B. Du Bois, *The Negro in the South* (Philadelphia: George W. Jacobs and Company, 1907), p. 24.

proved more potent for the slaves than those afforded by training in the manual arts and the hiring-out policy. They provided the indulged slaves with a greater number of significant others and left the slave personality less restricted to the plantation type. Probably of even greater historical importance is the fact that these opportunities encouraged the identification of these slaves with the master class and marked the birth of the Negro's aspiration for assimilation in a dominant white society. Two kinds of master-class relations illustrate the operation of these opportunities: the familial pattern that placed household servants in direct personal contact with their masters and outside the direct restrictions of the laws regulating slavery, and the direct formal training that came from the many close contacts between household servants and children of the master class.

Generally, the plantation was a large family whose affairs were directed by the master, the mistress, and the overseer. These three sought to control the lives of the slaves so that the maximum labor might be achieved. Discipline was stern, but of equal historical importance was the inevitable intimacy of association between the classes that came from nursing the sick, feeding the hungry, teaching the manual arts, and displaying an honest concern for domestic affairs.[41] Social intimacy between the children of the two races was seldom impaired by intense race consciousness, and social distance between the elements of master and slave classes varied to extremes in each direction. Joining the two groups, however, was a psychology of identification charged with an awareness of belonging together. Despite law or rule, the master possessed the power of widening the privileges of his slaves or of drawing restrictions more tightly about his neck. This was a "status" society in which the welfare of black men rested upon the mercy of white men who owned them.

[41] Francis B. Simpkins, *A History of the South* (New York: Alfred A. Knopf, 1956), p. 45.

Some slaves were fortunate to get their privileges extended far beyond the limits of local norms or even plantation regulations, for there were unpredictable circumstances that made this so. One of these, particularly, was the occasional threat of insurrection.[42] Masters found a good diplomacy in keeping some slaves closer to them than others in order that plans of insubordination and even rebellion could be more easily detected. To gain favor from the master or mistress, some slaves readily betrayed their fellow slaves even to the extent of inventing falsehoods about them. Rewards for these acts of treachery were so enticing that they encouraged the development of the "tattler" type of personality within the slave population. Out of such experiences came the tradition of tattling to whites—a tradition for which Negroes still criticize each other.

Nevertheless, the record shows that some masters were genuinely just and naturally humane. Austin Steward, a slave for twenty-one years, said of Colonel Alexander in 1859, "His slaves were always better fed, better clad, and had greater privileges than any I knew in the Old Dominion; and of course the patrol had long had an eye on them, anxious to flog some of those 'pampered niggers' who were spoiled by the indulgence of a weak owner."[43] Humanitarianism, however small, always left a lasting impression upon the slave's mind. Margaret Carpenter recorded in her recollections, "I well remember that, as a token of his good will, he [the master] always presented us [the slave children] with a slice of buttered bread when we finished our daily task."[44] Evidence of this childish appreciation of indulgence has been widely reported by other writers who have described plantation life. Harris Dickson characterized the humane interest of Colonel Woodville of Virginia by saying,

[42] For a complete survey of various slave insurrections in the South, see Herbert Aptheker, *American Negro Slave Revolts* (New York: Columbia University Press, 1943).

[43] Austin Steward, *Twenty-One Years a Slave and Forty Years a Free Man* (Rochester, N.Y.: Allings and Cory, 1859), p. 32.

[44] Margaret Carpenter, *Autobiography of a Female Slave* (New York: J. S. Redfield, 1857), p. 9.

"When the master returned from a journey, every human being on the plantation swarmed around him before he could shake off the dust. He had brought a present for every one. His pockets bulged with pen knives, band combs, tobacco, and gegaws."[45]

The practice of keeping personal servants close to the Big House and the aristocracy it sheltered was probably the most effective force in the informal education of Negroes during the slave period. It not only facilitated the reduction of social distance between master and slave, but also sponsored the development of refined personality traits within the slave population. Not all slaves lived in the plantation quarters. Some lived with their owners. In the court case of *Michan* v. *Wyatt*, the evidence showed that Leah Michan was very much attached to certain slaves and reared most of them in the dwelling with her own children. Evidence in the case of *Randall* v. *Long* revealed that a slave boy was born and reared in the family of the owner.[46] Although these are exceptional cases, a close relationship between master and servant was normal even in early Southern society. Some slaves slept in the same room with their masters in order to be handy for any need that would arise. Slave girls were almost constant companions of the little mistresses to whose whims they catered, and body servants were equally as inseparable from their masters who indulged them as a kind of luxury. Consciousness of the many niceties that went with being a household servant probably prompted Simon Phillips, ex-slave of the Bryant Watkins plantation in Alabama, to reflect, "Then there were the special privileges that made it so worthwhile being a servant on the old plantation."[47]

This kind of relationship was more than mere physical proximity. There was a closeness of mind involved, and social nearness helped to shape the slave's self-conception. Those who lived in the

---

[45] Harris Dickson, *The Story of King Cotton* (New York: Funk and Wagnall, 1937), p. 14.
[46] Sellers, *Slavery in Alabama*, p. 88.
[47] Armstrong, *Old Massa's People*, p. 34.

Big House judged themselves and defined their status in terms of such experiences. To be selected as a servant in the master's house was a source of pride; to be sent back to the fields was a source of humiliation.[48] In all the Southern states, field hands were regarded by slave and master alike as the lowest form of human bondage. The field hand's world was limited mainly to the quarters and the fields that stretched beyond them. His only stimulation from the outside world came through the relatively small collection of house servants who looked down upon him. Class lines between slaves of the same plantation were drawn, and this class consciousness was even extended to slaves of other plantations. Servants of wealthy and influential families were proud to be connected with greatness and power. They had little to do with their fellow bondsmen who were held by poorer and less conspicuous owners. Slaves of the more wealthy referred to themselves as belonging to "quality folks" and established within the Southern Negro population a tradition of looking down upon poor white people.

These special self-concepts and the behavior patterns that developed around them represented more than mere gestures of play acting. They were actual cases in which some Negroes, influenced by persistent intimacy with the master class, became like the quality folk with whom they identified. For example, Julie, the Negro nurse in the family of William Alexander Hoke, was reared and cultivated like the other girls of the Hoke family. She was married to a mulatto boy from the same plantation, and the ceremony was held in the Episcopal Church "in a big white-style wedding." Accepted as a family member by all the Hokes, Julie embarrassed the family and fell from grace when she later shouted in a Negro church. Master-class ways were often acquired by slaves through subtle suggestions and rather strict requirements. Neatness of dress and elegance of appearance quickly found their way into

[48] V. Alton Moody, "Slavery on Louisiana Sugar Plantations," *Louisiana Historical Quarterly* (April, 1924), 62.

the value systems of personal servants. Tawdriness of color and disheveled attire were not characteristic of all slaves of the servant class, for those whom they served were very particular about a servant's appearance. The women who served in personal attendance to a mistress were given sound advice along these lines.[49] Indeed, some of them learned so well that advising the little mistress about her appearance became one of their duties.

Manners and habits of the master class were copied with equal vigor and proficiency. In speech, many household slaves failed to develop a dialect of their own. Their tone of voice and use of words followed closely the pattern of their master and the members of his family. The entire dignity of the Big House was safe in their keeping. Assimilation in some instances was so complete that a slave could pass for white under the banner of master-class aristocracy, except when betrayed by his complexion or someone's knowledge of his previous condition. A mulatto slave girl, purchased at Louisville and reared on the Affleck Plantation in Texas, ran away to the nearby town of Brenham. There she registered in a hotel as a white woman. After receiving all the courtesies usually given an aristocratic Southern woman, she was pursued by her master and returned to the bondage from which she had temporarily escaped. Her aristocratic demeanor was never dropped; though sold to another family and married off to their servant, she was later emancipated and lived to serve as hostess to her former master who visited her at her home in Mississippi.[50] There were certain times when the Negro's ability to imitate the master class was employed as a source of amusement for local people. Such was the case of Jack Baker, servant to a Scotch merchant of Richmond during the first decade of the nineteenth century. Jack is said to have entertained the whole neighborhood through his practice of assuming

[49] Nemiah Adams, *Southside View of Slavery* (Boston: T. R. Marvin Sanborn, Carter, and Maine, 1855), p. 32.
[50] Thomas Affleck Papers, Reminiscences of Glenblythe, 1847–1866, Rosenberg Library Archives, Galveston, Texas.

the tone and manner of each of its aristocratic residents. Subjects of his imitative power, when concealed behind closed doors, were often surprised to "hear themselves" through the voice of the unsuspecting Jack. But Jack also got some private amusement from his imitative power. One of his best jokes was to call a servant in the tone of the servant's master and to disappear when the servant hurried to his master's bidding.[51] These incidents do not mark slavery as a bed of roses. They merely indicate that aspect of the institution which helped greatly to diffuse the Southern brand of American culture to favored members of the Negro population and gave them new conceptions of themselves.

Gradually and inescapably, indulgence led a select group of slaves to the printed page and later to the book. As Abigail Curlee concluded, many slaves learned less by precept than by example. They imbibed a good bit of this new type of culture from the voices they heard, the gestures and facial expressions they observed, and the habits of work they acquired.[52] Inherent in these experiences, however, were many chances for formal learning. A house servant learned from the master or mistress how to read and write or to distinguish among the different newspapers he was ordered to select, and Negro foremen learned enough to keep a daily record.[53] Such opportunities to gain literacy through more formal channels found their way into law. As early as 1762, North Carolina developed a law requiring that female mulattoes and colored apprentices be given instruction in reading by those to whom they were apprenticed. Female servants in the master's house were often expected to help young white children in the preparation of their school lessons. Since apprentices and slaves were made more useful by their ability to read, write, and do simple arithmetic problems,

---

[51] *Debow's Review*, 28 (February, 1860), 196–197.
[52] Abigail Curlee, "A History of Slave Plantations," *Southwestern Historical Quarterly*, 26 (July, 1922–April, 1923), 292.
[53] *Ibid.*, p. 285.

various attempts to repeal the North Carolina law failed in the Legislature of 1826–1827.[54]

That slaves did take advantage of these opportunities to begin their education is evidenced by the letters they wrote, the poetry they composed, and the general literary qualities they manifested. Albert Smith, a slave of Dr. Ashbel Smith, often wrote his master about being homesick when sent away for some purpose.[55] Moses, a slave on the plantation of James Pettigrew of North Carolina, was given the responsibility of managing several of his master's plantations. He kept his master informed of happenings through the many letters he wrote. Answering from White Sulphur Springs, Virginia, where he was apparently convalescing from some type of illness, the master chided Moses by writing, "As you succeed so well as a letter-writer, I must trouble you with writing more frequently. I wish you to send me a letter every other week and Henry every other week—which will enable me to hear from home every week."[56] When Robert Howell entered the University of North Carolina in 1856, he encountered the Negro poet, Horton, who had published a book of poems, and whom he considered "a historical character." In describing this character, Howell recorded, "He would write acrostics on the names of the boys' sweethearts for 25 cents. I patronized him liberally."[57] Out of Mississippi, late in the 1850's, came the distinguished Negro preacher and slave first known as "George." His literacy surpassed the point of being able to read the Bible and hymns, carrying into the general realm of

---

[54] Rufus E. Clement, "A History of Negro Education in North Carolina, 1865–1928," dissertation, Northwestern University, 1930, p. 4.

[55] Curlee, "History of Slave Plantations," p. 292.

[56] William S. Pettigrew to Moses (July 12, 1856). It seems that some Mr. White wrote letters for Moses, but that the slave himself composed them for dictation. For correspondence between Moses and his master, see The Pettigrew Papers, 1780–1900, Southern Historical Collection, University of North Carolina Library.

[57] Robert Phillip Howell Memoirs, 1856–1859, Southern Historical Collection, University of North Carolina Library.

scholarly familiarity with outstanding religious periodicals of his day. After hearing him preach twice in the courthouse of Pulaski, a noted lawyer remarked, "There is not a member of the Pulaski bar who could use better language, if compelled to speak so fast."[58]

The policy of giving slaves an opportunity to become literate reeled and staggered under the threat of law, but indulgence persisted. Alabama, in 1832, enacted a statute prohibiting the teaching of slaves to read and write, and practically every other Southern state did likewise.[59] These laws remained on the statute books until after the Civil War. Despite a general fear that literacy would expose slaves to abolition literature and stimulate them to revolt, a group of the South's religious leaders insisted that literacy was the potential savior of the South's system of slavery. Of these, none was more eloquent or persuasive than the Reverend George F. Pierce, Bishop of the Methodist Episcopal Church, South. In a sermon before the General Assembly of Georgia, March 27, 1863, the Bishop entered this plea for a tolerance of literacy among slaves: "The Negro is an imortal [sic] being and it is his right, by the law of creation and the purchase of his redemption, to read for himself the epistles of his Redeemer's love. If the institution of slavery cannot be maintained except at the expense of the black man's immortal interests, in the name of heaven, I say *let it perish.*"[60]

As men talked of laws and scriptures, the educative process afforded by indulgence continued. Opportunities for formalized instruction flowed freely into the slave population through the medium of estate inheritance. Leadership in this movement was often taken by white fathers of children born to their slave women.

[58] *Debow's Review*, 28 (March, 1860), 352–353.

[59] For laws prohibiting the teaching and assembly of slaves, see *Revised Code of the Laws of Virginia, 1819*, p. 425; *The Digest of the Laws of the State of Georgia, 1837*, p. 658; *Digest of the Penal Laws of the State of Louisiana, 1841*, p. 126; *Revised Code of North Carolina, 1854*, p. 219; and *Revised Code of the Statute Laws of the State of Mississippi, 1857*, pp. 247, 255.

[60] George C. Smith, *Life and Times of George F. Pierce* (Macon, 1888), pp. 474–475.

Carter G. Woodson reported that W. J. Morris acquired his education from his white father who was his master. Martha Martin's
daughter, born for her master, was sent to Cincinnati to be educated.[61] As early as 1789, Christopher Bean made a will providing
that his mulatto daughter, Venus, should receive a good education
and an equal dividend of his estate. On September 2, 1803, Charles
Fleming Bates, a Virginia attorney-at-law, executed a will providing that his slave daughter, Clemensa, should be free to every right
and privilege she could enjoy by the laws of Virginia, and he most
particularly directed that "she be educated in the best manner that
ladies are educated in Virginia."[62]

The "chum" relations that existed between household servants
and the children of their owners acted as an additional educative
force. In one way, these relations encouraged children of the master
class to teach the slaves through various kinds of "play schools."
Though starting in play, these schools were often taken seriously by
both "teacher" and "pupil." Such was the case on a Mississippi
plantation when a master's son, Virginius, aspired to make
"scholars" out of some of his father's slaves. He taught them in the
kitchen by the light of pine torches. Smedes reported that Virginius'
method of enforcing discipline of "these middle-aged men was truly
ludicrous." Following the example of his own teacher, he did not
spare the rod. As his own teacher had disciplined him, so did he
belabor the backs of his sturdy pupils at night. Five of his scholars
learned to read so well that they became preachers.[63]

Occasionally, this primitive educational system existed with the
master's blessings. Recalling her life as a girl in Virginia before the
Civil War, Letitia Burwell reported: "As soon as my sister and myself learned to read and cipher, we were inspired with a desire to

[61] Carter G. Woodson, *The Education of the Negro Prior to 1861* (New York:
G. P. Putnam's Sons, 1915), pp. 208–209.

[62] Helen T. Catterall, *Judicial Cases Concerning American Slavery and the
Negro* (Washington, D.C.: Carnegie Institute, 1926), III, 452–453, 119–120.

[63] Smedes, *A Southern Planter*, pp. 43–44.

teach the Negroes who were about the house and kitchen, and my father promised to reward my sister with a handsome guitar if she would teach two boys—designed for mechanics—arithmetic. Our regular system was every night to place chairs around the dining table, ring a bell and open school, she presiding at one end of the table and I sat at the other, each propped up on books to give us the necessary height and dignity for teachers. Our school proved successful. The boys learned arithmetic, and the guitar was awarded."[64] Richard Sinquefield, an African Methodist Episcopal minister who preached during the slave period, experienced similar educational advantages at the mercy of white children with whom he played. Born a slave in 1832, the property of the Reverend James Hogue of Butt County, Georgia, he was later sold to John Sinquefield. In recording his experiences with his new and indulgent master, the Reverend Sinquefield wrote: "The white children took great delight in teaching me how to read and write. I was an apt scholar and I learned right along. I would study at night from pine knots and burning greasy rags. I soon became a valuable man to my master. He trusted me with everything and I became his head man."[65]

But not all masters were quite so trusting. Many feared that a knowledge of reading in the head of a slave was equal to a key to freedom placed in his hand. Despite their opposition, however, the slave's desire to learn and the white children's desire to teach them remained strong. Master-class opposition merely drove the movement underground where it continued as a clandestine activity. The movement even operated within the household of the Honorable John Fouchereau Grimke, once colonel in the Revolutionary War and judge of the Supreme Court of South Carolina. His daughters, Sarah and Angelina, attended Sabbath School regularly and taught

[64] Letitia M. Burwell, *A Girl's Life in Virginia before the War* (Nashville: AME Sunday School Union, 1909), p. 22.

[65] *Life and Times of Reverend Richard Anderson Sinquefield, 1832–1908* (Nashville: AME Sunday School Union, 1909), pp. 7–8.

classes in the school for free Negroes during the afternoon. To this point their enthusiasm was tolerable, but Sarah allowed her zeal to get out of hand. She could not understand why a spelling book in the hands of a slave was a dangerous weapon, and she constantly fretted because she could only give her pupils oral instruction. She longed to teach them to read, for many of them were pining for the knowledge which, as she put it, "the poor white trash rejected." But she knew that the laws of the state not only prohibited the teaching of slaves, but also provided fines and imprisonment for those who ventured to indulge their fancy this way. So, argue as she did, the privilege of opening the storehouse of knowledge to the thirsty minds of black slaves was denied her. "But," she wrote, "my desire in this matter was not totally suppressed, and I took an almost malicious satisfaction in teaching my little waiting-maid at night, when she was supposed to be occupied in combing and brushing my little long locks. The light was put out, the keyhold screened, and flat on our stomachs before the fire, with spelling books under our eyes, we defied the laws of South Carolina."[66]

This underground movement to teach and learn grew stronger, and the spirit of defiance expressed by some of the white children spread to the slaves themselves. The life of John H. Thomas illustrates this fact as well as any other case one could cite. It is used here to show the basic manner in which a new self-conception and the aspiration to gain an education crept into the early lives of many slaves who were selected for some degree of indulgence on the part of the master class. Born a slave on the plantation of John Howes of Hanover County, North Carolina, John, the slave, developed a thirst for literacy that forty-three years of slavery could not quench. The thirst began while he was working in his master's store in Wilmington, for it was then that his mind was opened to the great value of the printed page—opened by a little

[66] As reprinted in Catherine H. Birney, *Sarah and Angelina Grimke* (Boston: Lee and Shepard Publishers, 1885), pp. 11–12.

white boy whose master had entered him as an apprentice clerk. Relating the incident in 1857 after his escape from slavery, John gave an extended account of how he, through bribery and trickery, employed his close relations with the planter class as a means of gaining literacy. Having received this advantage, he was able to pursue the freedom of self through a spelling book that became his constant companion.[67]

The literary zeal of Frederick Douglass was nourished in the same way. He, too, heard that knowledge would prevent his remaining a slave, and, like John H. Thomas, he made up his mind to get all that he could. His mistress, "miss Sophia," taught him to read the Bible, but was interrupted in this program by a husband who believed that "learning would spoil any nigger." Nevertheless, the boy who was to become one of slavery's most bitter enemies would not be denied. He turned the street into a school room and made his white playmates his teachers. He always carried Webster's spelling book in his pocket and kept bread enough to pay the hungry boys for giving him lessons.[68]

One can find many such cases of a slave's struggle to get an education and the courageous efforts of some white chum to help him along the way. Old slaves give mixed accounts of these educational escapades. In the experiences of some, learning was the expected thing—an apparently normal course of plantation life. For others, however, it was a forbidden and clandestine undertaking into which only the very young ventured.[69]

This theft of learning, whether with or without the assistance of white chums, transformed many slaves into what we traditionally know as self-made men. Lyell, reporting to the American Anti-

[67] *The Experiences of Thomas H. Jones* (Worcester, Mass.: Henry J. Rowland, 1857), pp. 13–15.

[68] See Benjamin Quarles, *Frederick Douglass* (Washington, D.C.: Associated Publishers, Inc., 1948), pp. 6–7; also Frederic May Holland, *Frederick Douglass* (New York: Funk and Wagnall, 1891), p. 15.

[69] Armstrong, *Old Massa's People*, p. 104.

Slavery Society in 1850 concerning his second trip to Alabama, noted that frequent mention was made of a Negro named Ellis, a blacksmith by trade, who had taught himself Greek and Latin. He was then in the process of acquiring Hebrew.[70] While on tour through parts of Georgia, E. P. Burke observed that, despite the precautions taken to prevent slaves from acquiring an education, many of them stole knowledge enough to enable them to read and write. Robert Smalls of South Carolina and Alfred T. Jones of Kentucky educated themselves in this word-stealing manner.[71] Thomas Fuller, a slave on a plantation near Alexandria, Virginia, had a genius for mathematics, and his feats in handling numbers won for him the title "Virginia Calculator." A party, including Dr. Benjamin Rush of Philadelphia, while passing through Virginia, heard of Fuller's fame as a mathematician and decided to test it. They asked him how many seconds a man seventy years, some odd months, weeks, and days had lived. Fuller gave the exact answer in ninety seconds. The man who questioned him took his pen and, after some figuring, told him he must be mistaken, that the number was too large. Fuller corrected him by saying, "Stop massa, you left out the leap years." Thomas Fuller, the Virginia Calculator, was correct.[72] Olmsted reported the case of a slave who was a carpenter in Montgomery, Alabama. The slave had developed remarkable mathematical proficiency without having been given formal instruction. He could give very close and accurate estimates for the quantity of all descriptions of lumber to be used in building a large dwelling. His master had purchased him for $2,000.[73]

These educational opportunities, like all the others that developed prior to the Civil War, were not available to all slaves. They

[70] *The Annual Report of the American Foreign Anti-Slavery Society*, May 7, 1850, p. 128.

[71] Carter G. Woodson, *The Education of the Negro Prior to 1861* (New York: G. P. Putnam's Sons, 1915), p. 207.

[72] Edward A. Johnson, *School History of the Negro Race in America* (Raleigh, N.C.: Edwards and Broughton, 1891), pp. 21–22.

[73] Olmsted, *Journey in the Seaboard States*, pp. 196–197.

were privileges extended by the more humane element of the master class, and they could be withheld more easily than they could be granted. Nevertheless, they did occur with sufficient regularity and over a broad enough scope to indicate the working of a natural force that pointed toward the eventual collapse of chattel slavery.

As slavery approached its end, certain signs of natural deterioration came vividly into focus. It became evident that the chattel concept could not be used to define entirely the relations between one human being and another. Even where the concept was employed to reinforce the economic relations between classes, economic efficiency repudiated it, and many slaves had to be trained as skilled persons in order to return a profit on the capital invested in them. Although their roles as servants were sharply defined in terms of broad social distances between themselves and those whom they served, the personal intimacy that crept into this service relationship slowly closed the distance until, in many instances, what was once a great chasm became a mere rift. The hidden passage had somewhat nullified the rationalism out of which American Negro slavery was born, and through it had passed many Negroes whose role in slave rebellions, abolitionary activities, or the anti-slavery movement was made more effective by their literacy and a sense of personal emancipation.

Anthropology and Negroes on the Southern Colonial Frontier

WILLIAM S. WILLIS, JR.

THE FIRST PART OF THIS ARTICLE is concerned with Negroes in the United States as a subject of study by North American cultural anthropologists. The second part introduces Negroes on our Southern colonial frontier as a subject matter for ethnohistory, a comparatively new subdivision of cultural anthropology. Because each part represents a departure from the mainstream of anthropology, our presentation is provisional and must contain error. However, we speak to provoke needful discussion and to stimulate needful research. The exposure of our errors is a small price to pay.

Cultural anthropology in the United States developed largely as a study of North American Indians. As political isolationism gave way to internationalism, anthropologists devoted increasing attention to Latin America, then to Asia, and finally to Africa. In making these shifts, anthropology in the United States was doing what Western anthropology in general has done, that is, the focus of anthropology has followed the national flag and the national currency.

When shifting to Latin America, anthropologists studied Negroes in Brazil and in the Caribbean Islands. Of course, they are now studying Negroes in Black Africa. This hasty review discloses one significant omission: cultural anthropology has largely ignored Negroes in the United States. Even Melville Herskovits, who did so much to develop Afro-American studies, devoted only minor attention to these Negroes.[1] The separate investigations of John Dollard and Hortense Powdermaker of the same rural community in Mississippi were singular and deviant manifestations of the broader interests that were developing in studying the acculturation of North American Indians and in studying quixotic communities in Western civilization.[2] The Dollard and Powdermaker monographs did not initiate any anthropological tradition that stressed the study of Negro culture in the United States. These monographs constitute mere exceptions that prove the rule!

Why anthropologists selected Indians instead of Negroes for study is an intriguing and important problem that has not been investigated. Indeed, it is seldom, if ever, seen as a problem. As far as is known, it is not the subject of a single article in the periodical literature. Moreover, it is ignored in the few histories of anthropology that now exist.[3] Yet this selection of subjects for study is obviously a major problem in the history of anthropology.

[1] Melville J. Herskovits, *The Myth of the Negro Past* (New York: Harpers, 1941).

[2] John Dollard, *Caste and Class in a Southern Town* (New York: Harpers, 1937); Hortense Powdermaker, *After Freedom: A Cultural Study of the Deep South* (New York: Viking, 1939).

[3] Alfred C. Haddon, *History of Anthropology* (New York: Putnam, 1910); Robert H. Lowie, *The History of Ethnological Theory* (New York: Farrar and Rinehart, 1937); Thomas K. Penniman, *One Hundred Years of Anthropology*

Possible explanations do exist. This selection was made in the nineteenth century and confirmed in the first years of the twentieth century. Since this is a complicated problem, one cannot expect a single explanation to be sufficient. The mystery of Indian origins led to an early fascination with Indians, which in turn led to a general intellectual interest in these aborigines. In addition, the explorations of the North American continent appealed to the prevalent natural-history tradition among Western scholars, which in turn directed attention to the Indians as a crucial feature of the indigenous phenomena of the continent. Viewed in this way, anthropology represents an academic specialization of this more generalized interest. This particular development did not exist with Negroes. The starting point was different. There was no mystery about Negro origins: Negroes came from Africa *via* the slave trade. Moreover, Negroes did not appeal to the natural-history tradition, since they were obviously not part of the indigenous environment. Finally, the conquest of the continent from Indian tribes has generally been seen as heroic, but the enslavement of the Negro people has provoked considerable guilt. Men laud heroism, but they avoid guilt whenever possible. These considerations point toward an explanation, but they go only a little way, for it should be recalled that other social scientists, mainly some historians and some sociologists, have studied Negro history and life.

Anthropology has focused on so-called aboriginal cultures of primitive peoples, that is, cultures unchanged by Western civilization. Some might say that this disqualified Negroes because they had assimilated so much of white American culture. It is true that anthropologists mainly sought only the most isolated and conservative Indian tribes and largely avoided the changes that had occurred in Indian cultures after the coming of the white man. How-

---

(London: Gerald Duckworth, 1952); H. R. Hays, *From Ape to Angel: An Informal History of Social Anthropology* (New York: Alfred Knopf, 1958); Marvin Harris, *The Rise of Anthropological Theory: A History of Theories of Culture* (New York: Thomas Y. Crowell, 1968).

ever, this explanation ignores the fact that no Indian tribe was really unchanged when first studied by anthropologists. On the other hand, it also ignores the fact that ex-slaves in the nineteenth century had a culture divergent from that of white America—a divergence sufficient to qualify Negroes as exotic subjects for anthropological study. Thus, anthropologists had the option of ignoring white cultural influence on Negroes as they did with Indians. Therefore, this explanation is not acceptable. It does, however, lead closer to the crucial answer.

To a large extent, modern Western anthropology is a by-product of capitalism and especially of capitalism in its imperialistic phase. This sad fact is beginning to be recognized, and anthropology is described increasingly as "the child of conquest" and "the child of colonialism." As such, anthropology has dealt with peoples beyond the boundaries of white populations, studying nonwhite peoples in the colonies.[4] Negroes and Indians were both nonwhite races, but Negroes were inside the boundary while Indians were outside the boundary. Moreover, the reservation can be seen as the functional equivalent of the colony of imperialism. This equivalence becomes even more precise when one looks at specialized colonies in Africa and Asia designed to contain conquered peoples who were neither an important source of unskilled labor nor an important market for the products of Western technology. In a similar way, most Indian tribes on reservations constituted an inconsequential sector in the economic system of the United States. Therefore, Indians fitted the image of the conventional subject matter of anthropology far better than did Negroes, but this is still not the crucial explanation.

Terroristic repression of Negroes was characteristic of the South after the Civil War. This repression increased by leaps and bounds after the so-called Compromise of 1877, which defined the Negro

---

[4] Claude Levi-Strauss, "Anthropology: Its Achievements and Future," *Current Anthropology*, 6 (April, 1966), 124–127; Kathleen Gough, "New Proposals for Anthropologists," *ibid.*, 9 (December, 1968), 403–407.

problem as a Southern problem. The North and the federal government now largely deserted the Negro. Since money for research has ulterior ends, the federal government and Northern philanthropy did not finance anthropological studies of Southern Negroes. Instead, these sources financed studies of defeated reservation Indians, who were still national wards. Those few Northern philanthropists, who still wanted to uplift the Negro, were not willing to risk Southern white anger for the sake of a mere exercise in scholarship. At this time, anthropologists were not interested in studying any kind of contemporary culture change. Moreover, these few philanthropists wanted to uplift the Negro by providing only a Christian education in self-help. This program was as much as the white South would tolerate. Therefore, even a mere exercise in scholarship by anthropologists was too risky to support, because anthropologists were becoming increasingly committed to antiracist explanations of cultural differences and to the methodology of field work. These new commitments meant that even an innocuous investigation of Southern Negroes struck at the very heart of the Jim Crow system of White Supremacy.[5] Had the sociopolitical picture and the financial situation been different, then the history of anthropology might very well have been different.

Despite the increasing commitment to antiracist explanations, anthropologists had little commitment to the Negro struggle for equality. The specific commitment to antiracism by the anthropologists from Europe, who were mainly Jews, was directed at the discrimination practiced by native-born white Americans against the new immigrants from Ireland and eastern and southern Europe. On the other hand, many native-born anthropologists continued to

[5] C. Vann Woodward, *The Strange Career of Jim Crow* (New York: Oxford University Press, 1955), pp. 49–95; Rayford W. Logan, *Betrayal of the Negro: From Rutherford B. Hayes to Woodrow Wilson*, 2nd ed. (New York: Collier Books, 1965); John Hope Franklin, *From Slavery to Freedom: A History of Negro Americans*, 3rd ed. (New York: Alfred Knopf, 1967), pp. 324–343, 382–412.

subscribe to racist explanations of sociocultural differences. Moreover, anthropologists in general were located largely in the North
and were not predisposed to get involved in the problem of Negro
rights. Apathy and hostility toward the Negro rapidly increased
in the North in the last half of the nineteenth century. Moreover,
many anthropologists were largely isolated from the problem;
they met few Negroes in their daily life in the North or on their
field trips in the West. Finally, one must consider the intricate
racism and escapism that led anthropologists to prefer reservation
Indians to shantytown blacks—even to "genteel" middle-class mulattoes. The anthropologists were not likely to lead their emerging science into competition with the older sciences of history and
sociology in studying Southern Negroes, especially when this
meant confrontation with powerful forces opposed to the Negro
struggle for equality.

The lily-white composition of anthropology now becomes per-
tinent. Negroes as anthropologists might have broken through this
neglect of Negroes; however, there were no Negro anthropologists
for a long time. It appears that a Negro was awarded a Ph.D. in
anthropology only in 1935 at the University of Pennsylvania, but
this scholar never participated in the mainstream of anthropology
in this country. It seems no other Negro received a Ph.D. until
1954 at Columbia University; then two more were awarded the
degree in 1955 at Columbia. Even today there are no more than
ten Negroes holding the Ph.D. degree in anthropology in the United
States.

This scarcity of Negroes in anthropology is not easy to explain.
Indeed, the scarcity requires as much research as any aspect of the
problem. Discrimination against Negro graduate students in departments of anthropology would perhaps have been less than that experienced by Negro graduate students in departments of history and
sociology. But, the opportunities for employment of Negro anthropologists were much less than those for Negro historians and Negro
sociologists, which is definitely one cause for the scarcity of Negro

anthropologists. However, the employment difficulty opens a new problem, since the vast majority of all Negro scholars was employed only in Negro colleges. The problem that now emerges is the failure of Negro colleges to provide teaching positions for Negro anthropologists. One reason is that most Negro colleges were in the South and refrained from risking Southern white anger and the withdrawal of financial support. However, another reason is suggested. Since Negro colleges were operated by and for middle-class mulattoes, values created by the privileged position of this subsociety did not incline its aspiring intellectuals to study anthropology. The anthropological preoccupation with Indians and backward primitive culture did not satisfy their commitment to the assimilation of white middle-class culture. Moreover, they did not see the relevance of this preoccupation to their daily struggles with discrimination and segregation. Therefore, they turned to history and sociology, where they have made important contributions to our scientific knowledge of Negro life and history. Indeed, the work of these mulattoes helps to sustain the present Black Revolution.

Anthropology is now responding to the present spreading discovery of the Negro by white scholars. This discovery can assist anthropology in its present struggle to survive in this revolutionary world by helping to change anthropology from its long preoccupation with relatively inessential matters (for instance, unusual prayersticks of the Pueblo Indians) to a concentration upon the more significant problems besetting men in this country and around the world.[6] Finally, this discovery of the Negro will attract more Negro intellectuals into the ranks of anthropology. In doing so, anthropology can overcome one of its greatest disadvantages in the contemporary world: being a lily-white social science that specializes in studying dark-skinned peoples who are now aroused.

On the other hand, anthropology has some advantages to offer

[6] Leslie A. White, "Anthropology 1964: Retrospect and Prospect," *American Anthropologist*, 67 (June, 1965), 629–637.

to the study of Negroes in the United States. At least, anthropology begins now without being unduly burdened by entrenched misrepresentations of Negroes. The anthropological field trip means living with people as a participant-observer, which can help the anthropologist overcome the middle-class bias that has often distorted investigations by sociologists and other social scientists of the Negro and of poor people in general.[7] In this connection, the anthropologist brings with him the perspective of many studies of Negro and other nonwhite communities in other parts of the world. Moreover, the crucial concept of culture and its derived concepts have been developed and used most expertly by the anthropologist. Finally, the anthropologist has at his disposal an emerging tradition that seeks the generalized pattern instead of the idiosyncratic event and seeks materialistic explanations of cultural phenomena instead of idealistic ones.[8]

The anthropologist who studies Negro culture of past decades and centuries becomes something of a historian. This anthropologist, known as an ethnohistorian, discards the field trip for the methodology of the historian. He remains an anthropologist, but he often asks different questions, for the document frequently does not give the same kind of data that field work does. To ask these new questions is a difficult task. It becomes a major difficulty when studying Negroes in the colonial South.

The ethnohistorian must learn more about documentary research. Too often the ethnohistorian has been amateurish. Historiography needs to become part of standard anthropological training. Professional contacts with historians need to become more common. However, before these innovations can occur, anthropology must

[7] Charles A. Valentine, *Culture and Poverty: Critique and Counter-Proposals* (Chicago: University of Chicago Press, 1968).

[8] Morton H. Fried, *The Evolution of Political Society: An Essay in Political Anthropology* (New York: Random House, 1967); Harris, *Rise of Anthropological Theory*.

overcome its bias against the "armchair" anthropologist and his library research.

A good starting point in reorienting anthropology toward Negro life and history is the Deep South in the eighteenth century. Until recent decades, most Negroes lived in this region. Since the Deep South in the colonial and early federal periods was the only place where Indians and Negroes met in large numbers, the transition in anthropological study from Indians to Negroes is made easier in this area of study. Moreover, the study of Negroes in the Deep South during those years encourages more communication between the anthropologist and the historian, particularly in view of the latter's traditional interest in Southern Negroes during the nineteenth century. On the other hand, anthropological interest in Southern Negroes in the eighteenth century should encourage historians to overcome their neglect of Negroes during this century.

Frontier conditions prevailed in the Deep South in the eighteenth century, despite the polished upper class in Charles Town, South Carolina. This frontier consisted of the seaboard white colonies and the inland Indian country. The white colonists included the English in the Carolinas and Georgia, the Spanish in Florida, and the French in Louisiana. The Indian country was inhabited by the Catawba, the Cherokee, the Chickasaw, the Choctaw, and the Creeks. This colonial South was an arena of an unremitting struggle for empire and trade among the white colonies, and the Indian tribes were caught in the middle of the struggle. Whites competed for their allegiance, for their trade, and for their warriors. Success in the empire struggle depended upon success in the Indian country.[9] Thus, the white colonies and the Indian country were locked in a basic interrelationship—a third dimension in which Negroes can be studied in the colonial South. The study begins with Negroes

---

[9] Verner Crane, *The Southern Frontier, 1670-1732* (Durham, N.C.: Duke University Press, 1928).

in this dimension and then moves easily to Negroes in the Indian country, avoiding the important problem of Negroes in the colonies, because research has been so very limited.

Some students, mainly Southern white historians, have stressed the small role that Negroes played among Indians and the great hostility that Indians showed toward Negroes. They seem to justify slavery and segregation by asserting that even the "savage" Indian despised the "beastly" Negro. Other students, mainly Negro historians, have stressed the importance of Negroes to the Indians and the prevalence of friendliness between the two groups. They are attacking oppression and expressing kinship with other nonwhites. After examining the documents, it may be concluded that the detractors of the Negro are more correct than the anthropologists. In the eighteenth century and especially before the American Revolution, Negroes were surprisingly unimportant in their participation in sociocultural institutions in the Indian country, and hostility was more pronounced than was friendliness. However, these detractors have not explained the causes of this unimportance or of this hostility. Perhaps they thought no explanation was necessary. These detractors have been surprisingly silent about the indirect repercussions that Negro slavery in the colonies had on sociocultural conditions in the Indian country. These oversights ought to stand correction.

The answer begins in the familiar story of divide and rule that has characterized white expansion and domination around the world. Indians outnumbered whites and so did Negroes early in the eighteenth century, and whites were afraid of these two nonwhite majorities. Their fear was realistic; for instance, slaves did rebel and Indians almost destroyed South Carolina in 1715. Whites were especially afraid that these two exploited races might combine against them. Moreover, they did not want the Indian country to become a sanctuary for fugitive slaves.[10]

[10] William S. Willis, "Divide and Rule: Red, White, and Black in the South East," *Journal of Negro History*, 48 (July, 1963), 157–176.

To prevent Indian revolt, South Carolina played tribe against tribe, even village against village. To prevent slave rebellion, South Carolina devised a harsh slave code and encouraged internal divisions among the slaves. To meet the nightmare of an Indian-Negro combination, whites deliberately maintained social distance between Indians and Negroes and created antagonism between them. To maintain social distance, whites had a basic rule: keep Indians and Negroes apart—do not let them mix. They tried to eliminate those situations where Indians and Negroes might establish close personal relations. Whites reduced the number of Indians in the colonies; they curtailed the enslavement of Indians and restricted the number of Indian visitors from the hinterland. On the other hand, whites tried to keep Negroes out of the Indian country and other out-of-the-way places. They had patrols on the roads and in the countryside. Ordinary citizens and even slaves were paid for capturing fugitive slaves. Finally, the Indians were paid handsome rewards for returning fugitive slaves—even dead ones. This policy of segregation, while not a complete success, achieved good results in keeping Indians and Negroes as strangers.

However, whites went further. They created antagonism by deliberately playing Indians and Negroes against each other. They pointed out that each was the enemy of the other. Then they went beyond propaganda to action. Whites used Negroes as soldiers against Indians and used Indians to catch runaway slaves and suppress slave revolts. At times, the whites simply encouraged Indians and Negroes to murder each other. In all these ways, whites played a big role in causing the scarcity of Negroes in the Indian country, the mutual racial antagonism, and the small direct influence of Negroes on sociocultural conditions among Indians.

However, this policy of divide and rule was only one cause. Geography was another. The Indian country was too far away and travel too difficult for many fugitive slaves. Many slaves simply did not know the way to the Indian country; at this time, most slaves were African born or only one generation removed. Moreover fleeing slaves were sometimes victims of the terroristic warfare practiced by the inland tribes. Once in an Indian village, Negroes might suffer from the whims of drunken Indians. Moreover, Indians sometimes deliberately betrayed the Negroes—often at the instigation of white agents and traders.

It is very probable that differences in culture between Indians and Negroes were equally important. They spoke different languages and not enough time had passed for English to become the lingua franca. Negroes came from West Africa and their native cultures were different and more developed than the existing Indian ones. The lack of cultural studies of eighteenth-century Negroes prevents any statement of greater precision. Moreover, exact knowledge of eighteenth-century Indian culture is not much better. For instance, disagreement now exists as to the inheritance of property and the succession to political office among the Indians.[11] Nevertheless, it is suggested that a different prestige system created misunderstanding and contempt. West Africans had the image of the farmer as the ideal man, whereas Indians had the image of the hunter as the ideal and considered farming as women's work. The obstacle of cultural difference between the two races was increased by the fact that more Negroes than Indians lived among whites and thereby assimilated more white culture than did the Indians. This difference was especially important in creating friction between Indians and fugitive slaves escaping to the Indian villages. It is suggested that a selective process favored the more assimilated Negroes of longer residence in the colonies instead of new arrivals from Africa and the West Indies, since the former had more opportunity to acquire the knowledge and equipment necessary to achieve successful escapes to the distant Indian villages.

Negroes, despite their experience in the higher cultures of West

[11] Fred Eggan, *The American Indian: Perspectives for the Study of Social Change* (Chicago: Aldine Publishing Company, 1966), pp. 15–44, 173–174; William S. Willis, "Patrilineal Institutions in Southeastern North America," *Ethnohistory*, 10 (Summer, 1963), 250–269.

Africa and in the white colonies, had little to offer Indians. Put another way: what Negroes had to offer, Indians seldom needed. Indians did not generally use Negroes as warriors, workers, traders, or advisors—especially since such use would provoke white anger. What Indians needed were more iron tools and munitions, things Negroes did not have. Finally, most tribes had some white traders whom they trusted as advisors. As we shall see, Negroes were more valuable as a commodity to be captured and sold.

The fear of Indian-Negro cooperation and the fear of the Indian country being used as a Negro sanctuary contributed to Indian survival in the eighteenth century. These fears partly explain why South Carolina adopted a policy of maintaining friendly Indians in the interior. South Carolina stopped its slave raids against the Indians and the enslavement of them, for the raids and enslavement were driving Indians to enlist the assistance of Negro slaves. Moreover, South Carolinians realized that a depopulated interior might be settled by fugitive slaves as long as whites were too few to settle this region. Some communities of fugitive slaves did appear early in the eighteenth century, and more existed during and after the American Revolution. News of these communities always created panic among whites, and top priority was given to the immediate destruction of these communities.[12]

There is some evidence that the fear of Indian-Negro cooperation and the fear of the Indian country as a Negro sanctuary persisted into the nineteenth century,[13] which suggests a new interpretation of the Indian Removal. This cruel relocation of the inland tribes

[12] Dunbar Rowland and A. G. Sanders, eds., *Mississippi Provincial Archives: French Dominion, 1701–1729,* 3 vols. (Jackson, Miss., 1927–1932), II, 573; Herbert Aptheker, "Maroons within the Present Limits of the United States," *Journal of Negro History,* 24 (April, 1939), 167–184; Willis, "Divide and Rule," pp. 161–165.

[13] Dunbar Rowland, ed., *Mississippi Territorial Archives, 1798–1803: Executive Journals of Governor Winthrop Sargent and Governor William Charles Cole Claiborne* (Nashville, Tenn.: Bardon Publishing Company, 1905), pp. 289, 366, 375–376.

to Indian Territory (now Oklahoma) by the Jackson administration in the 1830's is usually explained as a simple seizure of fertile soil for the expansion of cotton farming by Indian haters. Viewed in the present context, this explanation ignores the fact that the Indian Removal did not occur until whites were numerous enough to make a rapid occupation of the hinterland and therefore reduce the likelihood that an uninhabited area might act as a magnet attracting discontented slaves. Thus, the inland tribes became expendable, and the whites no longer had to live with the old fear of any Indian-Negro combination against them. More research into this matter is urged.

Reverting to the eighteenth century, one sees that the American Revolution marked a turning point in the role played by Negroes in the Indian country. Negroes as slaves became more common among Indians. The American Revolution permitted more Negroes to escape from the colonies, and Indians were then able to capture more fugitives in the wilderness. The British army gave slaves to Indians in return for their support, and Tories fled to the interior, bringing their slaves with them. The military resistance to westward expansion after the Revolution meant that Indians captured Negro slaves in their raids on white settlements.[14] At first, this increase in Negro slaves did not have a significant impact on economic production among Indians, for most did not know how to use slave labor efficiently. Indeed, they could not in their garden farming. Instead, the Indians became avid slave traders. Negro slaves were traded around the Indian country and then frequently sold back to whites. This was easily done. Since the Indian country was now surrounded by white settlements, Negroes captured in one direction were simply sold in another direction. Moreover, whites were so eager for slaves that no questions were asked.

---

[14] Benjamin Hawkins, *A Sketch of the Creek Country in the Years 1798 and 1799*, in *Collections of the Georgia Historical Society* (Savannah: Georgia Historical Society, 1848), III, pt. 1, p. 66.

Like the American Revolution, westward expansion of whites made it easier for more Negro slaves to escape safely into the Indian country. The Indian rule was that any fugitive slave making his way safely into an Indian village was a free man. Sometimes Indian greed and white pressure made Indians violate this rule and then Negroes were returned to slavery among the whites. However, occasionally this rule was not violated and the Negroes remained as free men among the Indians. In this way, a group of free Negroes gradually developed among the Indians.[15]

There now existed two subsocieties of Negroes—one free and one slave—in the Indian country. It seems that each subsociety had a somewhat different sociocultural identity. The free Negroes had made successful escapes from white slavery into the Indian villages. In general, this suggests the operation of a selective process favoring aggressive and brave personalities, which helps explain why some free Negroes played fairly prominent roles as advisors and warriors for Indians. Finally, it seems probable that these subsocieties became new means for the diffusion of both West African culture and white culture to the Indians. The Negro subsocieties as diffusion mechanisms in the Indian country constitute a major research possibility.

Although the Negro slaves did not have an immediate impact on economic production, a few Indian plantations based on Negro slave labor appeared early in the post-Revolutionary years. This plantation system spread in the closing years of the eighteenth century, and became the dominant socioeconomic institution in the early nineteenth century.[16] Constituting an exciting part of Negro experience in North America, this institution provides another variant for the comparative study of New World plantations,

---

[15] Willis, "Divide and Rule," pp. 171–173.

[16] Hawkins, *Sketch of the Creek Country*, pp. 66; Adam Hodgson, *Remarks during a Journey in the Years 1819, 1820, and 1821* (New York, 1823), p. 269; Henry Thompson Malone, *Cherokees of the Old South: A People in Transition* (Athens: University of Georgia Press, 1956), pp. 137–152.

a study that has been pursued by recent anthropologists.[17] Moreover, this institution will give anthropologists fresh examples and
probably fresh insights into problems of culture change. Many
documents exist that contain anthropological and other social science data about the plantation system and the participation of
Negroes in it. However, little is known about this institution, and
this ignorance is another unfortunate result of the neglect of Negro
life and history.

Nevertheless, one fruitful research problem can be suggested.
These plantations were controlled largely by mestizoes. Therefore,
it is important to know how mestizoes developed as a sociocultural
group and how they wrested political power from the traditional
war chiefs, who were largely fullblooded Indians. This political
struggle occurred during most of the post-Revolutionary years and
into the early nineteenth century. The spread and dominance of
the plantation system apparently were delayed until mestizoes won
their political struggle.

The picture given of the Indian country in the eighteenth century applies less to the Creeks and their Seminole offshoot. It appears that Negroes had a higher position among these two tribes.
More Negroes—free and slave—lived among the Creeks. Moreover,
these Negroes were more frequently advisors and warriors as well
as workers.[18] The Creeks lived in the path that Negroes used to
escape to freedom in Spanish Florida. Moreover, this location permitted the Creeks to trade with all white colonies, thus allowing
the Creeks more "balance of power" diplomacy. Whites, therefore,
did not have the same leverage to enforce their divide-and-rule
policy as they did with the other Indian tribes. Finally, the Creeks

[17] Vera Rubin, ed., *Plantation Systems in the New World* (Washington, D.C.:
Pan American Union, 1959).

[18] Thomas S. Woodward, *Reminiscences of the Creek or Muscogee Indians*,
Reprint (Tuscaloosa, Alabama, 1929), p. 108; Jedidah Morse, *A Report to the
Secretary of War of the United States on Indian Affairs* (New Haven, 1822),
p. 150.

maintained closer contacts with Spanish Florida and consequently had an additional model on which to pattern their relations with Negroes. The proportion of free Negroes among the Spanish exceeded that among the English. Also, the Spanish regularly used their Negroes—free and slave—to entice slaves from the English.

The greater service that Negroes performed for the Creeks influenced the Creeks to practice less racial discrimination against Negroes, and, therefore, racial prejudice was less developed. In turn, racial intermarriage was more common. Since most Negroes in the Indian country were males, these intermarriages were mainly phenomena of Negro males marrying Indian women. As the clans were matrilineal in descent, the mixed offspring became bona fide Creek citizens, and Negro genes spread easily and widely. This different situation of Negroes persists even today among the Creeks in Oklahoma.

In conclusion, a plea and a warning are in order. More anthropologists need to conduct more research on Negroes in the Deep South during the colonial and early federal periods. This must be done as quickly as possible, but not at the expense of high academic standards; despite the sense of urgency, scholars must strive toward accuracy, completeness, and objectivity. For instance, the struggle of Negroes for freedom and equality is obvious in the history of slavery and segregation. One need only mention the bravery of fugitive slaves. But, also important is the deeper struggle for mere survival under slavery and segregation, which in part explains why some Negroes captured fugitive slaves and sold them back into slavery. This stress on sheer survival condemns the oppression and exploitation of slavery and segregation no less than the stress on the struggle for freedom and equality.

Science demands that the current generation heed this warning. Prudence, also, demands this. Indeed, these demands are equal and complementary. The political forces in this country and in the world at large that have created the present preoccupation with Negro research are in a condition of delicate balance, which cannot remain stable. Change will occur, but in what direction? Despite good reasons for optimism, the realignment of political forces might ultimately be detrimental to present efforts. Perhaps money for Negro research will disappear and the element of fad will pass. If and when this happens, those who oppose racism in all of its forms must have created a solid block of knowledge about the Negro that can withstand the revisionist and racist counterattacks that then will surely come.

The Abolitionists

From Patience to Militance

ARTHUR ZILVERSMIT

IN TODAY'S RAPID REVOLUTION in race and race relations it is difficult to establish a sense of direction. Yesterday's certitudes are today's falsehoods and what once seemed to be a clear path is now confused and covered over. The seemingly united civil rights movement has disintegrated and a climate of mutual distrust and suspicion has clouded the "We Shall Overcome" spirit of only a few years ago. The optimism of 1954 has given way to despair. If historians had the power to predict the future, we would anxiously ask them to tell us where we are going. But, as we all know, historians cannot see into the future. They can, however, tell us how we got where we are and they can, by describing similar situations in the past, give us a clearer picture of present options. On the basis of historical knowledge, we cannot predict the future, but we can make more intelligent guesses as to the probable outcome of our responses to the challenge of our times. We can hope that an understanding of the past will help us to avoid the mistakes of the past.

In the hope, therefore, of not only illuminating the past but also casting some light on the problems of the present, we can explore another era and another confusing reform movement. The abolition movement was also dedicated to liberating black Americans and, like today's movement for black liberation, it too, had a bad press. It was derided as a movement of extremists—of bearded kooks who burned the constitution (instead of draft cards)—of men who had no sensible plan for eliminating the evil they opposed. The abolition movement of the 1830's, 1840's, and 1850's aroused in middle-class Americans—North and South—much the same sense of horror that today's protesters do.

But before the days of this more famous abolition movement, there had been another antislavery movement. The abolition movement of the era of the American Revolution has been neglected, but an examination of this earlier movement can help in making meaningful comparisons between moderate and militant reform movements. Let us compare the abolition movement that succeeded in ending slavery in the North with the later, more famous, movement that struggled to abolish slavery in the South.

Contrary to the common notion that the slaves of the North were only a few domestic servants, freed shortly after the restraining hand of Great Britain had been removed, it must be emphasized that slavery was an important economic and social institution in several of the Northern colonies and states. Although the slave population of New England was small, the Negroes of New York and New Jersey formed a significant proportion of the population on the eve of the Revolution. For example, the population of eighteenth-century Kings County, Long Island, was over one-third slave. Moreover, these slaves played a vital role in the area's economy. Although a few were employed as domestic servants, the overwhelming majority of Northern slaves, like Southern Negroes, were employed as farmers and craftsmen.[1]

Although slavery was a well-established, economically important institution, the abolitionists who sought to abolish it had certain advantages. To begin with, the era of the Revolution was friendly to reform. To the patriots, "the cause of America . . . [was] the cause of all mankind" and the American Revolution was to be "the birthday of a new world."[2] The American patriots saw their Revolution as more than a civil war within the British Empire—they saw it as a chance to establish in the New World a nation that would be proof of man's ability to create new and better institutions. The American Revolution, therefore, marked a secularization of the Puritan idea of mission, of America as a "City on the Hill" that would be a beacon to the rest of the world. By necessity, therefore, supporters of the Revolution had to undertake a reform of any imperfections in their society; Americans were forced to be reformers. Certain ages are particularly friendly to reform, and the American Revolution marked the crest of a reform-minded age.[3]

Not only was the Revolutionary era a period particularly hospitable to reformers, but the ideology of the Revolution was directly relevant to slavery. "Slavery" was a crucial concept in eighteenth-century political thought, and the connection between the political slavery the colonists were resisting and the servitude of the Negroes was obvious to all who chose to see it.[4] For example, "Anti-

---

[1] For a general discussion of slavery in the North, see Arthur Zilversmit, *The First Emancipation: The Abolition of Slavery in the North* (Chicago: University of Chicago Press, 1967), pp. 3–53.

[2] Thomas Paine, *Common Sense: The Complete Writings of Thomas Paine,* Phillip Foner, ed., 2 vols. (New York: The Citadel Press, 1945), I, 3, 45.

[3] Bernard Bailyn, *The Ideological Origins of the American Revolution* (Cambridge: Harvard University Press, 1967), pp. 230–319.

[4] *Ibid.,* pp. 232–246. For a perceptive analysis of the relationship between opposition to slavery and enlightenment thought, see David B. Davis, *The Problem of Slavery in Western Culture* (Ithaca: Cornell University Press, 1966), pp. 341–445.

Slavetrader," who wrote in a Pennsylvania newspaper in 1768, pointed to the inconsistency of slavery with the new concern for the rights of man. He taunted the patriot slaveowners, "You who spurn at the thoughts, of paying a poor pittance of a glass, a paper, a paint tax, and cry aloud on freedom and virtue, how can you lift your heads in the noble contest for Liberty, and at home be the greatest tyrants on earth!"[5] After the Declaration of Independence, abolitionists pointed to its eloquent statement of libertarian principles and demanded, "If these . . . are our genuine sentiments, and we are not provoking the Deity, by acting hypocritically, let us apply earnestly and heartily to the extirpation of slavery from amongst ourselves."[6]

The new hostility to slavery was reflected in a series of petitions to the state legislatures, asking for gradual abolition laws that would provide for the emancipation of the children of the slaves. Gradual abolition was debated in almost every Northern state legislature during the war, and Pennsylvania, Rhode Island, and Connecticut enacted gradual abolition laws by 1784. Vermont abolished slavery in her constitution of 1777, while the new constitutions of Massachusetts and New Hampshire were interpreted by the courts in such a manner that slavery rapidly disappeared in these states.[7]

In New York and New Jersey, where slavery was firmly entrenched, the abolitionists fought their hardest battles. Faced with the obvious fact that the Revolutionary elan was not enough to ensure the abolition of slavery in these states, the antislavery men began to organize. The Pennsylvania Society Promoting the Abolition of Slavery, which had been founded in 1775, but had lapsed during the war, was revived in 1784. Although slavery had already been put in the process of extinction through the gradual abolition law, Pennsylvania abolitionists sought improvements in the law and hoped to influence the abolition movement in other states. New

[5] *Pennsylvania Chronicle*, November 21, 1768.
[6] *Independent Chronicle* (Boston), October 3, 1776.
[7] Zilversmit, *First Emancipation*, pp. 109–153.

Yorkers formed the New York Manumission Society in 1785, and a few years later New Jersey abolitionists, with considerable aid from the Pennsylvania society, organized a New Jersey antislavery group.

These societies prepared petitions, which they presented to state legislatures and to Congress. They asked for laws for gradual abolition and for the protection of slaves and freed Negroes. They also supported schools for freed blacks, helped them to find employment, and supervised their morals, hoping to confute those who argued that Negroes were incapable of using their freedom in a constructive way. In 1794, a national convention of antislavery societies was called to co-ordinate these activities.[8]

The abolitionists who organized these societies were remarkable in many ways. Working within the context of the ideology of the American Revolution, they had aims not remarkably different from those of many of their neighbors. Like other Americans, they hoped to make their nation strong—they wanted it to be a better place than any spot in the Old World. They saw themselves as in the mainstream of American society. They "knew" that their principles would eventually triumph. And because they knew that time was on their side, they were remarkably patient men. They were convinced that if the state legislature did not adopt their proposals in one session, then perhaps they had better try again the next year. They were convinced that "the voice of reason, and the impulse of humanity . . . [would] gradually tend to the emancipation of the slaves."[9]

Not only were the abolitionists themselves patient, but they counseled patience to the enslaved Negroes and urged them to submit quietly to the commands of their masters. By patient acquiescence, the abolitionists pointed out, not only would the slaves be immediately rewarded by better treatment, but their

[8] *Ibid.*, pp. 162–167, 173–175.
[9] *Minutes of the Proceedings of a Convention of Delegates from the Abolition Societies* . . . (Philadelphia, 1794), p. 13 (hereafter, *Convention Minutes*).

masters might also become convinced of the injustice of slavery.[10] Similarly, in the wake of Gabriel's slave revolt in Virginia, the abolitionists expressed their disapproval of insurrections.[11] Freedom should come from the convictions of the whites, not the violence of the blacks.

Because they believed they had a real chance to influence their legislatures, the early abolitionists were anxious not to give unnecessary offense and they were extremely cautious and prudent. In 1798, when the revolt of the Negroes of Santo Domingo alarmed many Americans, a convention of antislavery delegates pointed out that "a peculiar degree of caution" was now necessary and that the abolitionists should consolidate the gains they had already made, rather than attempt any new ventures.[12] The antislavery men were equally cautious in managing their own societies—after extended debate and long consideration, the New York Manumission Society refused to bar slaveholders from membership and its president, John Jay, continued to own slaves.[13]

Because they were basically in harmony with the aims of America, they had no desire to unduly upset the status quo, and the plans for emancipation supported by the abolitionists were remarkably moderate and conservative, calculated to appeal to all but the most closed-minded defenders of slavery. As the New Jersey abolitionists pointed out in their petition to the state legislature, "We ask . . . for no *law* to touch property *in possession* . . . We supplicate you for the *unborn* . . ."[14] The abolitionists of the Revolutionary era asked only for gradual abolition laws—laws that would eliminate slavery by freeing

10 *1798 Convention Minutes*, p. 18.

11 *1801 Convention Minutes*, p. 38.

12 *1798 Convention Minutes*, p. 11.

13 New York Manumission Society, "Minutes," New York Manumission Society MSS, New-York Historical Society, I, 16, 29, 36, 40, 56; William Jay, *The Life of John Jay*, 2 vols. (New York: Harper, 1833), I, 335.

14 *The True American* (Trenton), February 6, 1804.

the children of slaves. These laws would not emancipate any living Negroes and therefore would not infringe on a master's property rights. Moreover, the abolitionists agreed that the children of the slaves who would be freed by the gradual abolition laws would have to spend many years in the service of their mothers' masters, to repay them for the cost of raising the children. In all respects the gradual abolitionists paid careful attention to the rights of property, and none of their proposals envisaged a sudden or radical change in race relations or in property rights.

These cautious, patient, and prudent reformers were respectable men. They represented in general the members of "the establishment." For example, Benjamin Franklin served as president of the Pennsylvania Abolition Society. A later president of the society, James Pemberton, was a leading Quaker merchant and a member of one of the most distinguished Pennsylvania families. The New York Manumission Society included on its rolls Alexander Hamilton and John Jay. Men who were active in securing the freedom of Massachusetts Negroes included the important Federalist leader, Theodore Sedgwick, and a future governor of the state, Levi Lincoln. The Connecticut abolition society enrolled Jonathan Edwards, Jr., and Theodore Dwight, another leading Federalist politician. The president of the New Jersey Abolition Society, Joseph Bloomfield, had been a general in the Revolutionary War and later served as governor of the state. The abolitionists of the Revolutionary era, it is clear, represented the most respected classes in society. This was no small group of outcasts; this was no displaced middle class; these men were the real leaders of society.[15]

[15] Membership of the abolition societies can be determined by consulting their minutes. Besides the records of the New York Manumission Society, cited above, the papers of the Pennsylvania Society for Promoting the Abolition of Slavery are located at the Historical Society of Pennsylvania, in Philadelphia, and the manuscripts of the New Jersey Society for Promoting the Abolition of Slavery are in the Quaker Collection of the Haverford College Library in Pennsylvania.

As might be expected of a reform movement made up of so many representatives of the upper classes, the tone of the abolition movement was very much *noblesse oblige*. Negroes were considered the proper objects of charity, the clients of the philanthropic abolitionists, but blacks were not members of the abolition societies. Often the blacks were treated as children to be protected, watched over, and guided, but not to be consulted or listened to. The abolitionists spent a great deal of time and effort in giving advice to the freed Negroes, urging them to lead upright and moral lives, to avoid drinking, gambling, and other vices. For example, the New York Manumission Society appointed a special committee to promote reform "among that part of the African race, who are dissolute in their morals, keep houses of ill fame, and are otherwise pursuing a conduct injurious to themselves and others."[16] The freed blacks did not always accept the advice of their white patrons. When the abolitionists told the freed Negroes of New York that their proposed celebration of the end of the African slave trade might be too noisy and thereby reflect on both the Negroes and the abolitionists, the freed blacks indignantly rejected this gratuitous advice and went on and had their party, just as they had planned.[17]

Even when freed Negroes organized in order to promote abolition, they could not always count on the wholehearted support of the white abolitionists. Pennsylvania free Negroes, for instance, petitioned the state legislature for a total abolition bill and offered to pay a special tax to compensate the masters of their enslaved brethern. But the Pennsylvania abolition society opposed this plan. The white abolitionists opposed the bill for several reasons, including the fact that the free Negroes would not be able to pay a special tax without great hardship.[18] While the abolitionists were undoubtedly correct in this assumption, the argument reflected their

16 New York Manumission Society, "Minutes," II, 181.
17 *Ibid.*, II, 223, 231.
18 *Claypoole's American Daily Advertiser* (Philadelphia), February 10, 1800; Pennsylvania Society for Promoting the Abolition of Slavery, "Minutes," II, 16.

attitude toward the Negroes as children to be protected and guided rather than as partners in a common enterprise.

There is no evidence, however, that differences between whites and blacks involved matters of basic ideology. Richard Allen, the founder of the A.M.E. Church, for instance, echoed the sentiments of white abolitionists when he counseled the slaves that "patient waiting" was necessary before freedom and that the slaves should put their "trust in God."[19] Jupiter Hammon, the slave poet of New York, urged slaves to obey their masters, not only because this was God's command, but because obedient slaves could expect better treatment. Although Hammon acknowledged that liberty was desirable, yet, he added, "Getting our liberty in this world, is nothing to our having the liberty of the children of God."[20] Massachusetts and Connecticut Negroes who petitioned for their emancipation were also cautious. Connecticut Negroes, for instance, pointed out that, although they knew they had a natural right to freedom, yet they recognized that "it is not best for us to use violent measures."[21] Massachusetts Negroes, in a similar petition, promised that while they awaited their freedom they would continue to "be obedient to our Masters."[22]

Although antislavery men of this era—black and white—in general advocated a cautious gradualism, a few recognized that slaves had every right to win their freedom by violent means if necessary. Theodore Dwight, a Connecticut abolitionist, argued that, if war was ever justifiable, then the slaves must be justified in resorting to violent means to attain freedom. He asked, "Who . . . can charge the negroes with injustice, or cruelty, when 'they rise in all the

[19] Richard Allen, "To the People of Color," *The Life Experiences and Gospel Labors of the Rt. Rev. Richard Allen* (Philadelphia, 1887), p. 72.
[20] Jupiter Hammon, *An Address to the Negroes in the State of New York . . .* (New York, 1787), p. 14.
[21] Herbert Aptheker, ed., *A Documentary History of the Negro People in the United States*, paperbound ed., 2 vols. (New York: The Citadel Press, 1962), I, 11.
[22] *Ibid.*, I, 7.

vigour of insulted nature,' and avenge their wrongs? What American will not admire their exertions, to accomplish their own deliv-
erance?" Dwight declared that gradual abolition was not enough—
if, as he believed, the slaves were entitled to liberty, then immediate
abolition was the only honorable course.[23] Another radical on this
issue, Abraham Bishop, defended the actions of the Negroes of
Santo Domingo who had revolted against slavery. "Let us be consistent," he urged Americans; "if we justify our own conduct in
the late glorious revolution, let us justify those, who, in a cause
like ours, fight with equal bravery."[24] But these views were exceptional. The overwhelming tone of the antislavery movement of the
late eighteenth century was nonviolent and moderate.

The gradual abolitionists were rewarded for their efforts. For
them, patience and moderation paid off. Pennsylvania improved its
gradual abolition law and New York and New Jersey passed gradual abolition laws in 1799 and 1804. Although their successes were
not repeated in the South, the gradual abolitionists continued for
many years to believe that the same methods that had worked in
their states would succeed in the South. But the gradual abolitionists had never been strong in the South, nor were their views popular. Jefferson knew the views of most Virginians and he never saw
an opportunity to even present his gradual abolition plan.

With the triumph of gradual abolition in the North, many of the
early abolitionists retired from the cause—they did not see much
chance of influencing legislatures outside their own states. The only
way in which they believed they could help the movement for abolition in the South was by supporting the activities of the American
Colonization Society, which seemed to offer a means for ending
slavery by sending the freed slaves out of the country. By 1830,

<hr/>

[23] Theodore Dwight, *An Oration Spoken before "The Connecticut Society, for
the Promotion of Freedom and the Relief of Persons Unlawfully Holden in
Bondage"* (Hartford, 1794), pp. 23, 8.
[24] [Abraham Bishop], "Rights of Black Men," *American Museum,* XII
(1792), 300.

however, it had become clear that the South was not inclined to abolish slavery and that the colonization would not lead to emancipation. By 1830 the hopes of the gradual abolitionists that their movement would spread to the South had obviously proven false and the stage was set for a new, militant antislavery movement.

The new abolition movement that began in the 1830's—the antislavery crusade of William Lloyd Garrison, Frederick Douglass, Henry Highland Garnett, Theodore Weld, and John Brown—differed markedly from the earlier movement in tone and direction. Garrison set the tone for the new movement in the first issue of his newspaper, *The Liberator*. He promised: "I will be harsh as truth, and as uncompromising as justice. On this subject, I do not wish to think, or speak, or write, with moderation. No! no! Tell a man whose house is on fire to give a moderate alarm; tell him to moderately rescue his wife from the hands of the ravisher; . . . but urge me not to use moderation in a cause like the present. I am in earnest —I will not equivocate—I will not excuse—I will not retreat a single inch—AND I WILL BE HEARD."[25]

The new movement—especially the followers of Garrison—specialized in a vituperative brand of journalism. It differed also from the earlier movement in its ability to get involved in a sometimes irrelevant purism—a purism that led to abundant quarrels among abolitionists and a sometimes astonishing irrelevance to the broader issue of how best to abolish slavery. Garrison, for example, measured all existing institutions in terms of their relationship to slavery. Viewing the Constitution as a document that compromised with slavery, he publicly burned it and refused to participate in any government organized under its provisions. Seeing the churches as hopelessly contaminated because they refused to expel slaveholders, he denounced them fiercely and refused to have any dealings with them.

[25] Wendell Phillips Garrison and Francis Jackson Garrison, *William Lloyd Garrison, 1805–1879*, 4 vols. (New York: The Century Co., 1885–1899), I, 225.

Although Garrison rejected the gradualism of the early abolition movement and substituted a cry for immediate abolition, he did not reject the earlier movement's faith in reasoned persuasion, nor its faith that the principles of abolition would eventually triumph. Unlike the earlier movement, however, the Garrisonians did not attempt to influence legislatures to pass abolition laws, but rather concentrated on trying to convince individual slaveholders that they sinned in keeping slaves and to persuade them to emancipate their Negroes. Accordingly, the main role of antislavery organizations, according to Garrison, was "MORAL AGITATION" dedicated to achieving "a MORAL REGENERATION." Garrison would use the same methods as Christ's apostles had used to spread an earlier truth— "the foolishness of preaching."[26]

This emphasis on the conversion of the slaveholder and the attempt to persuade him to end slavery by setting his Negroes free— this emphasis on loving the sinner while hating the sin—often led to strange conclusions. Garrison, for example, said that because the Constitution supported slavery he would not vote, even if his vote would be the one needed to free every slave in the nation.[27] Another abolitionist put the issue even more clearly: "The question," he said, "is not so much how we shall abolish slavery as how shall we best discharge our duty . . . to ourselves."[28] The great concern for purity of motives and means could, and did, lead to an astounding irrelevance and a socially useless privatism.

This concern for finding ways to "keep our skirts clean of this iniquity,"[29] was not the only trend in the new abolition movement.

---

[26] William Lloyd Garrison, "Exposition of the Anti-Slavery Platform . . . ," *Platform of the American Anti-Slavery Society* (New York, 1855), pp. 14–15.

[27] For Frederick Douglass' amazed reaction to Garrison's remarks, see Phillip Foner, ed., *The Life and Writings of Frederick Douglass*, 4 vols. (New York: International Publishers, 1950–1955), II, 351–352.

[28] Quoted in Gilbert H. Barnes, *The Antislavery Impulse, 1830–1844*, reprinted (Gloucester, Mass.: Peter Smith, 1957), p. 101.

[29] "Resolutions Adopted by the Reformed Presbyterians . . . ," *American Anti-Slavery Society, Annual Report, 1856–1857*, pp. 89–90.

An obscure black man of Boston, David Walker, was not restrained by pacifism or nonresistance. Writing with a fiery sense of indignation, he predicted that unless the whites reformed immediately and freed their slaves, a terrible slave rebellion would accomplish God's purpose of liberty. He urged the slaves, ". . . if you commence, make sure, work—do not trifle, for they will not trifle with you . . . if there is an *attempt* made by us, kill or be killed."[30] Henry Highland Garnett, a young black Presbyterian minister, told a Negro convention in 1843 that the need for violence was clear. In direct contrast to Bishop Allen and Jupiter Hammon, who had urged the slaves to endure patiently and had told them that God commanded slaves to obey their masters, Garnett told the slaves that rebellion was a duty. "IT IS SINFUL IN THE EXTREME," he argued, for Negroes voluntarily to submit to the degradation of slavery. In clear, unequivocal language, Garnett called on his enslaved brethren to "Strike for your lives and liberties. . . . *Rather die freemen than live to be slaves.* . . . It is in your power," he pointedly remarked, "so to torment the God-cursed slaveholders that they will be glad to let you go free."[31] Frederick Douglass, the most famous of the black abolitionists, had begun as a Garrisonian, rejecting violence. By 1849, however, Douglass told a Boston audience that he would "welcome the intelligence to-morrow . . . that slaves had risen in the South, and that the sable arms which had been engaged in beautifying and adorning the South were engaged in spreading death and devastation there."[32]

As the Civil War approached, the possibilities of violence as a means for ending slavery appealed to more antislavery men. Wendell Phillips, although clearly identified with the nonresistance wing of the abolition movement, heartily endorsed John Brown's raid on Harpers Ferry. Even William Lloyd Garrison was moved,

[30] David Walker, *David Walker's Appeal, in Four Articles* . . . , Charles M. Wiltse, ed. (New York: Hill and Wang, 1965), p. 25.
[31] Aptheker, *Documentary History*, I, 229, 232.
[32] Foner, *Douglass*, I, 338–339.

finally, to declare that he wished "success to every slave insurrection at the South."[33] The new antislavery movement that began in the 1830's was clearly different from the movement of the Revolutionary era. But, why was one movement concerned with the elimination of an evil institution relatively moderate, cautious, and even respectable, when at a later date a movement concerned with eradicating the same evil was radical and militant?

In answering this question, it is important to re-emphasize the role of revolutionary ideology as the context for the first abolition movement. There are certain eras when reform is popular and when the reformer can attract a large audience. The first abolitionists did not act like an embattled minority, because they did not feel they were in fact a minority. They believed that their principles were true, and such was their faith in human progress that they could not imagine their principles would not soon triumph. In 1795, for example, the antislavery convention observed that many men acquiesced in permitting slavery "merely from want of reflection" and argued that "if to such were often applied the force of reason . . . they might be awakened to a sense of their own injustice."[34] Although the Garrisonians at first continued to believe that moral suasion would convert the slaveowner, this belief foundered when the South refused to heed the advice of the abolitionists and, what was worse, began to defend slavery as a positive good. The earlier abolitionists were patient because they thought time was on their side and reform was inevitable, because they thought that only a small prod was needed to move the larger society to reformation.

A second reason that the earlier abolitionists were so moderate was because of their view of slavery. They viewed it as an evil and even as a sin, but, in general, they viewed it as an evil that could easily be removed. For them slavery was an incidental evil, one

[33] Quoted in John L. Thomas, *The Liberator: William Lloyd Garrison* (Boston: Little, Brown and Co., 1963), p. 397.
[34] *1795 Convention Minutes*, pp. 28–29.

that could be eliminated without any major surgery on the body politic. Like moderate reformers of another era—the Progressives —their basic outlook on life was optimistic and cheerful, and they saw the United States as a country that would grow in virtue as time went on. Only yesterday the Americans had been content to be British subjects. Today they were free, and tomorrow their Negroes would also be free. Later abolitionists, however, were unable to take this view of slavery. Their view of slavery as a sin, coupled with a belief in the possibility of total redemption, led to a demand for immediate repentance from sin and immediate abolition.[35] They viewed slavery primarily as a moral problem and, as Garrison pointed out, in times of moral danger—when a ravisher threatens —moderate relief is not sought. Furthermore, they saw slavery no longer as incidental, but as totally corrupting the society that tolerated it. As Frederick Douglass put it, ". . . the whole system, the entire network of American society is one great falsehood, from beginning to end." For him "slavery [was] . . . interwoven with the very texture—with the whole network—of our social and religious organizations."[36] With this view of slavery as being a basic evil, woven into the very structure of society, moderate reform became impossible.

When slavery was thought of as an institution that corrupted the whole country, the abolitionists could no longer rely on other institutions, because they had been irrevocably corrupted. While the earlier abolitionists worked through church and state to effect their ends, the later abolitionists could not. As Frederick Douglass asked,

---

[35] The relationship between revivalism in religion and immediatism in the abolition movement is described by Barnes, *Antislavery Impulse*. The change in the ideological context of the earlier and later abolition movements is brilliantly explored by David B. Davis in "The Emergence of Immediatism in British and American Antislavery Thought." This article, along with a number of other relevant items, is reprinted in David B. Davis, ed., *Ante-Bellum Reform* (New York: Harper & Row, 1967).

[36] Foner, *Douglass*, I, 207, 216.

"To what institution, to what party shall we apply for aid? . . . Shall we go to the Church for this influence? . . . Shall we go to politicians or political parties?"[37] Not only did the relative weakness of institutions in the America of the Jacksonian period mold the abolition movement, but also the total unavailability of sympathetic institutions led to a rejection of the formal institutions of the society.

Finally, the harshness of tone, the threats of violence, and also the privatism of the later abolition movement were a product of the fact that America would no longer listen to abolitionists. Men like John Jay and Benjamin Franklin did not have to worry, as did William Lloyd Garrison, whether they would be heard. They did not have to shout or make extreme statements to secure an audience. They already had the ear of the decision makers and, therefore, they had a stake in moderation; harsh language was more likely to alienate their audience than to widen it.

Because Americans had not followed the advice of the gradual abolitionists and eliminated slavery in every corner of the nation, they were forced to face a different abolition movement at a later date. Having rejected the pleas for moderate, gradual reform, America was forced to deal with demands for total and immediate reform. As the intransigence of America society became more and more evident to the later abolitionists, they became more and more convinced that slavery was not just a superficial blemish, but a deep cancer that corrupted the whole of American society. In this way, every piece of evidence that American society would not respond to the urgency of the reformer's vision reinforced the reformer's radicalism. As Henry Highland Garnett surveyed the utter failure of the abolitionist movement before his day, he drew the conclusion that we had come as far as we could using the means of the past:

---

[37] *Ibid.*, I, 237. For an interesting discussion of the relationship between abolitionism and anti-institutionalism, see Stanley Elkins, *Slavery: A Problem in American Institutional and Intellectual Life* (Chicago: University of Chicago Press, 1959), pp. 140–206.

". . . the cause apparently waits for a more effectual door to be thrown open . . ." And open it he did.[38]

The frustrations experienced by the abolitionists as slaveowners and politicians refused to listen to them and to heed their pleas for reform led to two trends within the later abolition movement. In some men it led to a greater preoccupation with the moral obligation of the reformer—the failure of society to respond to the urgency of their vision led to an excessive concern for self-righteousness, an excessive privatism. In what seemed to them to be a totally immoral world, these men occupied themselves with making their inner world a "clean, well-lighted place." Having been denied an audience that would respond to their arguments, meeting a wall of opposition they could make no impression upon, they turned inward. Since neither the tone nor the content of their argument had the slightest influence with their audience, they had no reason to moderate their tone or to compromise their views and every reason to use only their own consciences as guides to what they said. They sometimes became more concerned, therefore, with having made the morally correct statement than with having made a contribution to the abolition of slavery—and this was understandable. It seemed that they *could* make no real contribution to ending slavery, while they could at least satisfy the demands of their own consciences.

For other abolitionists the frustrations of their situation, the frustrations engendered by not having an audience that would respond to reasoned argument, led to the conclusion that a society so immoral, so impervious to reasoned argument, was not worth saving and had to be destroyed. They were led finally to a commitment to violence as a substitute for reason. Therefore, both the excessive concern for meeting the demands of private conscience and the demand for radical, violent change stemmed ultimately from the intransigence of a society that had failed to listen to the arguments of moderate reformers.

[38] Aptheker, *Documentary History*, I, 230.

The Hidden Freedmen

Five Myths in the Reconstruction Era

WILLIAM S. MC FEELY

ONLY TWICE SINCE THE END OF SLAVERY have white Americans even come close to wanting for black Americans what black Americans wanted for themselves.[1] One occasion was the Civil Rights movement of our own times. The other was the Reconstruction era.

[1] Black and white Americans worked together politically in the Populist era but a recent study of Kansas Populism suggests that the goals of the allies were fundamentally different. Most Negroes sought protection from violence and the status that political patronage could bestow, while white Populists sought economic restructuring of the society (William H. Chafe, "The Negro and Populism: A Kansas Case Study," *The Journal of Southern History*, 34, no. 3 [August, 1968], 402–419).

During this twelve-year period from 1865 to 1877 some former slaves became independent farmers; state conventions in which black men served as active delegates drew up liberal constitutions; black people gained the vote; and colored politicians participated in the governing of the South and the nation as judges, state legislators, congressmen, and senators. The legal base for equality, erected during Reconstruction, remained, although much of what these men helped build upon it was later torn down. The Fourteenth Amendment, in defining the rights of all citizens, brought the word *equal* into the Constitution, and the Fifteenth forthrightly acknowledged what divided the nation by declaring that no man should be denied his vote "on account of race, color, or previous condition of servitude."

In all, Reconstruction was a crucial period in the Negro's struggle for equality. Yet, the way the story is often told leaves the impression that Reconstruction proved equality to be a very poor idea. Most accounts of the period—whether popular legend or scholarly text—reflect the nation's thinking during those long periods (longer than the two mentioned) when racial inequality was the governing belief. Such an assumption made it psychologically necessary for white Americans to see the Negro in Reconstruction as a man very different from the one he was.

Some black Americans, out of profound disillusionment, have distorted the story also. The black man has been a realist in America because he has had to be; only rarely has he abandoned a cold hard appraisal of his world. He did so in looking back at Reconstruction. Hopes were so high then that it was painful to look squarely at their destruction. It is almost too much to ask of black people that they remember how hard their forefathers worked to achieve equality during Reconstruction. To do so is to require them to accept that un-American condition, failure. Reconstruction did not succeed. As one historian, who was black and who did face the failure without flinching, noted in speaking of Reconstruction in

1901, "For this much all men know: despite compromise, war, and struggle, the Negro is not free."[2]

Less perceptive historians and sociologists have subscribed to the "we were not ready yet" view of the strenuous attempts to gain equality by a people whose efforts demonstrated that they were indeed ready.[3] As the excerpt from "Of the Dawn of Freedom" suggests, W. E. B. Du Bois made no such mistake. He argued strongly that an honest look at black accomplishments during Reconstruction would encourage a belief in equality. But he knew, also, that Negroes must look just as closely at what had blocked them on their road to freedom, if that way were ever to be opened fully to them.

During Reconstruction the freedmen—men who had recently been slaves—made a claim on the nation to rebuild itself so that they could have a better life than they had known under slavery. Some things in their way of life they wanted to keep; others they wanted very much to change. They did not want things to go on as they had under slavery. This was what the freedmen wanted and, whether they liked the idea or not, other Americans at the time understood the word Reconstruction in the same way. Only when the nation gave up this experiment, denied the Negroes' claim on the federal government for help in their advancement, and abandoned the freedmen to sharecropping and to having their way of life defined by white Southerners, did Reconstruction become a dirty word.

It was the abandonment of that effort, and not Reconstruction itself, that left the legacy of racial problems facing the nation today. Refusing to look at the era, as one might hide a traumatic personal recollection, is no help in the solution of these problems. Indeed, present purposes are sometimes served by candidly owning up to

---

[2] W. E. B. Du Bois, "Of the Dawn of Freedom," *The Souls of Black Folk*, (New York: Fawcett, World, 1968), p. 41. The essay was originally published as "The Freedmen's Bureau," *Atlantic Monthly*, 87 (March 1901).

[3] For a statement of this view see Henderson H. Donald, *The Negro Freedman* (New York: H. Schuman, 1952).

past troubles and Americans, black and white, who are trying to figure out where they stand in relation to each other might well examine Reconstruction. There may be value in looking realistically at another time when, though men failed, they tried to reach each other.

To achieve this frank look, it is necessary to cut through the myths that have gathered over Reconstruction as a protective cover for those who do not want to face the facts. Five such images that have hidden the freedmen need particular attention: (1) the myth of the Day of Jubilee, (2) the myth of the Exodus, (3) the myth of the Prodigal Son, (4) the myth of Forty Acres and a Mule, and (5) the myth of the Menacing Black Man.

The first myth, the Day of Jubilee, tells the story of slaves gathered on the lawn of the plantation to learn from the Union army captain or from Ol' Massa himself that they are slaves no more. In this portrait the Negroes are childlike, overemotional people waiting passively for a deliverer and shouting hallelujah when he comes. The picture of the tear-stained face of the grateful emancipated slave seems to document an image of the "darkies" as simple folk. It confirms their affecting gratitude to their emancipators; it suggests, as well, that they are not a people who will struggle to make it on their own, in the manner of other ethnic groups in America.

Getting a true idea of what this moment of recognition meant to the man just freed is difficult. Most slaves were illiterate; it was illegal to be otherwise, and few letters exist describing the moment. Drawing on their sense of the past, novelists have given us their guesses. Margaret Walker, in *Jubilee*, writes, "Brother Ezekiel was a very sick man. . . . He seemed to be dying. . . . 'I was just laying here praising the Lawd. I thank God I done see the year of Jubilee. Now . . . I can pray "Lord lettest now Thy servant depart in peace." . . . Mister Lincoln is our Moses and God done told him to make old Pharaoh set my people free.' " Miss Walker senses a profound experience of release. She may or may not be right in her decision to cast its expression in the rhetoric of the Bible. But even if she is right on both these points, it seems unlikely that many freedmen were willing to follow Brother Ezekiel and celebrate Jubilee Day by dying. Indeed, the novelist proves she is skeptical of her own interpretation; she has one of the brother's visitors correct him, " 'but old Pharoah ain't never done no such thing yet.' "[4]

The freedmen knew their troubles were not all behind them. They approached the opportunities and dangers of freedom in the same skeptical and practical spirit with which on a day-to-day basis they had striven to ameliorate their condition under slavery. Even the short period of looting and the burning of cotton gins by the freedmen on the sea islands after their masters left does not prove mass irrationality on the part of ex-slaves in America. There is, after all, a certain logic in their delivering a swift kick to the device that had secured King Cotton's throne. More important, these freedmen soon gave up stealing from their masters' houses, symbols of what cotton profits could bring, and instead began raising cotton of their own as independent farmers.

Freedom meant not release from responsibility but rather that now there was something worth working for. When the Emancipation Proclamation came, Negroes in the South quickly learned that it did not end slavery. What it did do was convert a white man's war into a war to change the way of life hated by black people. Some freed Negroes resisted impressment into the Union army as an unacceptable slavery-substitute but, given the chance to enlist, others did so in great numbers.[5] In all, approximately 200,000 Negroes, or about 10 percent of the Union army, served as soldiers to see that the war was won and freedom secured. For these men there was no Jubilee Day; instead there were days and days of infantry duty.

Northerners who had been working with the freedmen in cap-

---

[4] Margaret Walker, *Jubilee* (Boston: Houghton Mifflin, 1966), pp. 242–243.
[5] Willie Lee Rose, *Rehearsal for Reconstruction: The Port Royal Experiment* (Indianapolis: Bobbs-Merrill, 1964), pp. 146–147.

tured parts of the South were also skeptical of Jubilee Day celebrations. They watched in April 1865 as William Lloyd Garrison, the most famous of the abolitionists, and Henry Ward Beecher, the greatest preacher of the day, led a delegation to Charleston to celebrate the raising of the stars and stripes over Fort Sumter. Beecher's son-in-law makes it clear that this became one of the greatest of Jubilee celebrations. "In the morning went to Zion Church, a large building capable of holding 3,000 and it was crammed. . . . A sprinkling of white officers & ladies in front near the Pulpit, the rest of the audience negroes of every size, sex, color, age & size." Beecher's preaching was never stronger: ". . . emotion began to work in the audience like the rising of the wind in the forest or the sobbing of the waves upon the Beach. . . . Tears streamed down the faces of black & white alike. Again another would burst out into laughter while another would break out with 'Thank you massa, Glory to God'—"[6]

This sermon, and the response of the freedmen to it, dismayed Gideon's Band—a nineteenth-century peace corps that had been working with the freedmen on the islands off the Carolina coast since their capture in 1861. The governor of this experiment in educating the freedmen was Rufus Saxton. He did not go to the Charleston celebration and did not like the idea of the freedmen being encouraged in the view that freedom was swapping one master for another. Instead, somewhat tartly, the tough Unitarian urged the visiting Yankee liberators not to put too much faith in jubilation. There was still a lot of work to be done training the former slaves to be independent farmers. Saxton invited the Beecher party to come out to see how the "freedmen are living on their new farms."[7]

For many of the slaves of these islands, the first experience of

[6] Samuel Scoville to Harriet Beecher Scoville, 17 April 1865, Beecher Family Papers, Yale University Library.
[7] Rufus Saxton to Henry Ward Beecher, 18 April 1865, Beecher Family Papers.

freedom was one of decision. Sam Mitchell remembered as a little boy hearing the booming from the Union gunboats and watching his family's master desperately pleading with his male slaves to row him back to Charleston. The boy's mother and father had to decide quickly whether to risk freedom. The decision was made: said Sam's mother to his father, "You ain't gonna row no boat to Charleston, you go out dat back door and keep a-going."[8] This choice of freedom was the way the little boy always remembered the day.

Not all the slaves were as lucky as the Mitchells in having their masters abandon them. For most of the four million freedmen Ol' Massa was still right there in the spring of 1865. And he wanted to get a crop in the ground as he always had at that time of the year. Although the freedmen may have believed that things had changed, the discussions about planting that spring may not have been as different as the end of slavery might lead one to suspect.

On June 6, 1865, three Mississippians in Attala County signed a contract penciled on a scrap of paper. It was witnessed by Union army officers: "This is to certify that we were present and this day witnessed a contract between J. W. Simmons and negroes (Calvin R. & Febe) which he lately owned—and that the substance of Col. Young's order was told to them informing them of their freedom and that they could hire themselves to whomever they chose but that said freedmen agreed to remain and work for said Simmons for their rations and clothing in the usual way before the war."[9] Whatever may have been Calvin R. and Febe's private feelings of jubilation on hearing Colonel Young tell them they were no longer slaves, they were faced with the reality of going about their lives as they had always done. Granting the enormous release of knowing they could no longer be separated by sale, they nevertheless had to look forward to working in the fields under the same discipline

---

[8] Rose, *Rehearsal for Reconstruction*, p. 12.
[9] Contract on file, RG 105, Bureau of Refugees, Freedmen, and Abandoned Lands, National Archives, Washington, D.C.

they had known in slavery. The rewards were also the same—a cabin, clothes, and food: just what they had always been.

The conditions reflected in these contracts suggest that the response of the freedmen to freedom was coldly pragmatic. That there are so few Negro accounts of irrational jubilation may not stem from an inability to write—more than a few could—as much as from the fact they did not feel jubilant. Those accounts of emotional outpourings that we do have may in part be the product of the ex-slaves responding as men like Beecher and Garrison expected them to. Calvin R. and Febe and their children did not live in a world of Moses or of reformed Pharaohs. And even up-to-date liberators went back home to the North, leaving Calvin R. to cope with the familiar J. W. Simmons and an unfamiliar army officer on hand to keep order.

Calvin R. and Febe's response to being told they were free does considerable damage to the second of the Reconstruction myths as well. They stayed where they had always lived; they did not set off for the River Jordan. The myth of a vast biblical Exodus of the freedmen has had its adherents among black story tellers as well as white ones. Some Negroes have hoped to see in this movement of the freed people a quest for a wholly new way of life. Some white tellers of the tale seem to be suggesting a symbolic suicidal parallel to the theory put forth by white supremacists during Reconstruction, that the Negroes, unequipped to be free men, would die once freed.

One of the most trenchant interpreters of black people of the South was William Faulkner, but even he could falter on the treacherous ground of Reconstruction. Here is his telling of the exodus:

They began to pass in the road yonder while the house was still burning. We couldn't count them: men and women carrying children who couldn't walk and carrying old men and women who should have been at home waiting to die. They were singing, walking along the road singing, not even looking to either side. They didn't even settle for two days, because that night they passed: we sat up listening to them, and the next morning every few yards along the road would be the old ones who couldn't keep up any more, sitting or lying down and even crawling along, calling to the others to help them; and the others —the young strong ones—not stopping, not even looking at them. I don't think they ever heard or saw them. "Going to Jordan," they told me. "Going to cross Jordan."[10]

This chapter in *The Unvanquished* ends with a vast multitude of black people pressing toward a bridge that gives way. They keep pressing, still singing their hallelujahs, and drown in the river.

Faulkner's picture of the slaves moving lemminglike into the River Jordan is derived in part from fact. There were thousands of black people on the roads of the South during the Civil War, but they were refugees—unarmed civilians—fleeing cavalry units of both armies. In Faulkner's own northern Mississippi, which was Calvin R. and Febe's as well, the Union and Confederate armies fought back and forth across the land with a terrible ferocity, and the black people were the civilians who suffered most. Those who fled did so to save their lives, not out of some mindless death-wish.[11]

Although there was a high mortality rate among the refugees, the figures for the survivors do not suggest an exodus. The black population of Memphis, the Yankee-held goal of most of the refugees in the Faulkner area, rose only from 3,882 in 1860 to 15,828 in 1865.[12] In areas not fought over, there was, during the war, no group movement of the Negro population. Labor shortages in Texas and in Louisiana did produce considerable movement of freedmen after the war, but there was no Civil War–era demographic shift

[10] William Faulkner, *The Unvanquished* (New York: New American Library, 1958), pp. 103–104.

[11] John Eaton, Jr., *Grant, Lincoln and the Freedmen* (New York: Longmans, Green and Co., 1907), p. 30.

[12] U.S. Census Office, *Population of the United States in 1860* (Washington, D.C., 1864); David Tillson, Report of Freedmen's Bureau Census of Memphis and Vicinity, 18 August 1865, RG 105, National Archives.

anything like the great migration of the twentieth-century blacks from the rural South to the urban North.

A second version of the Exodus story—one more congenial to black listeners than Faulkner's—sees the movement of freed people as an expression of a back-to-Africa movement. In this version, the freed slaves want to turn their backs on all they had known of slavery and go on to something entirely different. They are pictured as wanting to found a new world—a settlement in some uninhabited place—or desiring to find again the lost world of Africa.

Emigration figures do not reveal the Reconstruction era as a time for back-to-Africa. The American Colonization Society was eager to have it become such and called on the Freedmen's Bureau to use its offices all across the South to advertise Liberia and to use its large transportation appropriation to move the freedmen across the ocean to that country. The Bureau was indifferent and so were the freedmen. Only 2,494 of the 4,000,000 Negroes of the South moved to Liberia between 1865 and 1870.[13]

If there was little return to a lost fatherland, neither was there abject dependence on that famous father-figure, Ol' Massa, celebrated in the myth of the Prodigal Son. This is the story not of a group exodus, but of the individual slave who is told he is emancipated and to celebrate goes off on a drunken spree. You will recognize him as the ancestor of Daniel Patrick Moynihan's irresponsible Negro male who deserts his family and leaves to his woman—to the matriarch—the responsibility for whatever family stability there may be. Slavery, it is alleged, taught the slave little about family life.[14] Free as the wind, Sambo took off without a care

[13] Willis Boyd, "Negro Colonization in the National Crisis, 1860–1870," Ph.D. dissertation, University of California, Los Angeles, 1953, p. 309.

[14] *The Negro Family: The Case for National Action*, Office of Policy Planning and Research, United States Department of Labor (Washington, D.C.: U.S. Government Printing Office, 1965), p. 15; Stanley M. Elkins, *Slavery: A Problem in American Institutional and Intellectual Life* (New York: Grosset and Dunlap, 1963), p. 55.

in the world. Then comes the morning after; sober and wiser he comes back to his old plantation, begs forgiveness of "massa" and "missy," and docilely goes to work.

Several things are wrong with this story. First, as noted, there was less movement than this legend assumes. Most freedmen, like Calvin R., never went away at all. Second, those who did go to the city often went explicitly to seek a job.[15] Third, many of the freedmen who did travel (not the war refugees) did so not to escape their families, but to put them back together. Explaining the roaming, Bureau agents reported that many freedmen were looking for "Kin Folks," and the Negro *New Orleans Tribune* carried long lists of lost relatives believed to have been sold to owners in Louisiana.[16] Often the only address for these undeliverable messages was "James" or "Liza"—little help in finding lost relatives but proof of a poignant sort that out-of-sight out-of-mind was not a universal attitude of slavery.

The experience of Calvin R. and Febe is also suggestive of a firmer family structure continuing out of slavery. On thousands of labor contracts it was the male head of the family who signed his name, or his mark, for himself, for the other workers in the family, and, to cite Calvin's case, for his "dependents: George 9 years, Joe 5 years, Tomas 4 years." Thus, as members of a family, they remained where they had always lived.

Those freedmen who did go off, for whatever reason, often returned but not in the manner of the biblical prodigal son. The

[15] Observers who point to a high number of freedmen vagrants often overlook the fact that the "vagrancy principle" was being practiced to maintain labor discipline in a postslavery society. Individuals, sometimes holding jobs, were arrested in towns as vagrants and escaped jail only by agreeing to contract to work as field hands. Willemina Kloosterboer, *Involuntary Labour since the Abolition of Slavery: A Survey of Compulsory Labour throughout the World* (Leiden: E. J. Brill, 1960), chap. 3; William S. McFeely, *Yankee Stepfather: General O. O. Howard and the Freedmen* (New Haven: Yale University Press, 1968), p. 168.

[16] James Scott Fullerton to O. O. Howard, 28 July 1865, RG 105, National Archives.

freedman came back not to the father-figure in the big house but to the mudsill of his own cabin. Slave quarters seemed squalid to outside observers, but these observers may have missed the importance the huts held for their inhabitants. Modern sociology tells us something about this. Appalled by slum conditions, city planners have leveled decaying buildings for high-rise replacements. Dreary bug-infested flats disappeared but so did the security of life on the block. Too late it was discovered that the bad old neighborhood could sustain the inhabitant as well as dismay the observer.

It is possible that the slave quarters on a plantation may have served a similar function. The cabin not only provided respite from the painfully fatiguing and excruciatingly boring work of the fields, but also represented distance from the discipline of the master. Seventy-five years after he had been freed, a Louisianian named William recalled that the "quarters was a little piece from the big house, and they run along both sides of the road that go to the fields. All one-room log cabins, but they was good and warm, and every one had a little open shed at the side where we sleep in the summer to keep cool."[17] In the hut and the patch around it, the man living in slavery could produce all that he could call his own. The patch may have produced little in the way of food but it was familiar and it was the base from which the freedman hoped to build his new life in his new condition of freedom. It was to this familiar cabin and patch that a free man, and not a prodigal son, returned.

This return to the familiar complies perfectly with the realities of the freedmen's problems perceived by Rufus Saxton and other concerned Northerners. They saw a farm as a necessity if the freedmen were to provide for their families and to get a start on their own. If the patch could be extended to include enough land for a self-sustaining farm, the freedmen would be off to a sound

---

[17] Charley Williams in B. A. Botkin, ed., *Lay My Burden Down* (Chicago: University of Chicago Press, 1968), p. 112.

beginning. Both the attachment of the black farmer to his own hut and patch and the conviction of his white allies that he deserved such a start as a free man, led to the idea of forty-acre land grants. And yet, ever since Reconstruction, Negroes have been accused of naively—even childishly—believing in an unfounded myth of Forty Acres and a Mule. The mule aside, it was no myth; it was an act of Congress.

Even before the Civil War was over, Congress, on March 3, 1865, enacted the Freedmen's Bureau Bill and instructed Commissioner O. O. Howard to divide all the lands abandoned to Union armies in the South into farms of forty acres and to distribute them to freedmen families. The command of the Congress was so explicit that Howard had to get a ruling from Attorney General Speed in order to use town properties for hospitals and other nonfarm uses.[18] Although there was only enough land abandoned to provide for twenty thousand freedmen families, the act put the federal government clearly on record as favoring land redistribution in order to make the freedmen independent farmers.

In the summer of 1865 the Freedmen's Bureau established application procedures for the lands and widely advertised their availability across the South. In spite of this beginning of an implementation program, which raised great hopes among the freedmen, almost no lands were distributed to them. President Andrew Johnson energetically pardoned former rebels and in August 1865 declared that with a pardon should go restoration of all lands. By executive action he nullified an act of Congress. Before Congress reconvened in December, virtually all the lands had been restored and none were available to the freedmen.

In the fall of 1865, President Johnson sent General Howard on a tour of the South to convince the Johnsonian all-white state governments that the Freedmen's Bureau would see to it that the blacks, who would be disappointed not to get their forty acres, would not

18 McFeely, *Yankee Stepfather*, p. 99.

get out of hand. While he was on this tour, Howard spoke to the freedmen as well. As he spoke, he converted the Freedmen's Bureau from an agency with great potential for achieving basic social and economic change into just one more voice of white paternalism. He pleaded with the freedmen to sign contracts to work in field gangs, as if the supervision of these contracts by the Bureau agents would make field-gang labor as attractive to the freedmen as owning their own farms. He told them to depend on their former masters to be kind and urged them not to jeopardize the gains they had made—emancipation—by pressing for equality. And above all, Howard told them, they must give up the myth that they would be given forty acres, "à la mode Santa Claus," as another Bureau official mockingly put it.

The freedmen ignored Howard's advice about not pressing their claims vigorously. They did step forward and this activity gave birth to the Reconstruction version of the myth of the Menacing Black Man. In Louisiana, in November 1865, the colored community ran a mock election to demonstrate its capacity and desire to vote. In the city of New Orleans, their man got more ballots than the regularly elected governor, but their impressive demonstration did not bring enfranchisement. Therefore, on July 31, 1866, they staged another demonstration of their eagerness for the vote. Behind an American flag and with a band—very likely an excellent one—they marched to the Mechanics Institute where a somewhat irregularly convened Constitutional Convention was to meet to consider black suffrage.

On the way, the marchers were heckled, a fight began, and shots were fired. (It will never be known who fired first.) When the marchers reached the Institute, the police arrived and fired on them and drove them away. Then, on the grounds that the convention was a disturbance to the peace, policemen and firemen stormed the upstairs meeting chamber. As black delegates and those white members of the convention known to favor Negro suffrage fled down the stairs, they were shot and beaten to death. That night white bands attacked black neighborhoods killing and burning. When General Philip Sheridan—no bleeding-heart liberal—arrived from Texas, he declared the repression "a massacre."

Congress agreed. The mayor of New Orleans was a political ally of President Johnson's, and his law enforcement officials had given a vivid demonstration of what home rule meant to the blacks of the South. To the Republicans in Congress, as eager as the President to build political support in the South, the way to stop the lawless attacks on the Negroes was to remove the Johnsonian governments. In their place, Negroes were given the vote and they, and white politicians willing to work with them, drew up new constitutions and then proceeded to elect legislators, governors, and congressmen, representative of a new interracial constituency.

This radical or black Reconstruction of the South proceeded progressively. That the new state constitutions were not replaced when Reconstruction was ended is proof of their workability. These legislatures laid the foundation of the South's public school system and enacted other long-due measures, such as penal reform. And yet the activities of the black politicians in these legislatures gave Reconstruction the reputation for being a threat to the nation. The reason: the Menacing Black Man. This is a myth older than Reconstruction and it cannot be adequately treated here. Historians are notoriously squeamish on matters sexual, and the writer is as cowardly as the rest. However, the profession should pay a little more attention than it does to what most men in the street claim, rather unclearly, to be the real issue. Luckily, the part that Reconstruction played in the creation of this myth can largely be discussed in political terms.

The first four mythical views of the freedmen on their Jubilee Day, in the Exodus, returning as a Prodigal Son, or conjuring up a dream of Forty Acres and a Mule, all served to fix an image in the white nation's mind of the Negro as a simple child. Perhaps he was troublesome, but essentially he was harmless. The fifth myth suggests the opposite. Now the black man is a direct threat to white men in areas that white men claimed as their own.

The most influential teller of this legend was a Northerner and an abolitionist as well. Troubled by the cruelties of slavery, James Shepherd Pike of Maine had worked to see slavery abolished. In 1873, he took a trip to South Carolina to see what he had wrought.[19] Here is the way he described his visit to the South Carolina legislature in a book widely read in his own day and influential in pictures of Reconstruction from the film *Birth of a Nation* down to textbooks in use today.

> Yesterday, about 4 p.m., the assembled wisdom of the State . . . issued forth from the State-House. About three-quarters of the crowd belonged to the African race. They were of every hue, from the lightest octoroon to the deep black . . . Every negro physiognomy was here to be seen. . . .
>
> It is the dregs of the population habilitated in the robes of their intelligent predecessors. . . . It is barbarism overwhelming civilization. . . . It is the slave rioting in the halls of his master. . . .
>
> [It is] a Black Parliament, . . . the only one on . . . earth which is the representative of a white constituency. . . . The Speaker is black, the Clerk is black, the doorkeepers are black, the little pages are black, the chairman of the Ways and Means is black, and the chaplain is coal-black.[20]

For Pike, Carolina had become the "Congo"; "amalgamation" threatened his future. And most white Americans agreed with him. When white Southern redeemers used murder and intimidation to force the Negroes to either support white supremacy or withdraw from politics altogether, the North did not stop them. When Adelbert Ames, the integrationist governor of Mississippi, in 1875

---

[19] John Sproat observes that Pike had this derogatory picture in mind before he went South in 1873. John Sproat, *The Best Men: Liberal Reformers in the Gilded Age* (New York: Oxford University Press, 1968), p. 35.

[20] James Shepherd Pike, *The Prostrate State: South Carolina under Negro Government* (New York: D. Appleton and Company, 1874), pp. 10, 12, 15.

reported to President Grant that he needed troops to end a grue-
some series of pre-election killings of blacks in that state, Attorney
General Edwards Pierrepont replied rather wearily, "The whole
public are tired of these annual autumnal outbursts in the South."[21]
No protection for the freedmen was provided and, with the Compromise of 1877 two years later, the Negroes were abandoned
completely by the federal government and left to have their way of
life determined by white Southerners. The menace of the black
man was ended; he was forced back into agricultural serfdom.

Historians can help in setting the facts straight on how much
of a threat the black politician posed during Reconstruction. Readers who are timid and pale can rest assured; first, there was no
black take-over. Only in South Carolina in one session of the lower
house was there a black majority. In no state was there a black
governor. Legislative committees and the boards of public agencies
governing hospitals and universities, as well as the courts, were
integrated, but nowhere was there black predominance.

Second, there is no evidence that the black legislators deported
themselves in a way that could be called threatening or, indeed,
that they were more eccentric than their white predecessors. Surely
there was a shift in tone when a man who had just learned to read
stood up to give a speech from a desk where once sat a tidewater
aristocrat. But a republic that had survived Andrew Jackson's
unruly inaugural might have been expected to survive the assault
on its tastes of another voice from the people.

Third, the endlessly repeated charge of corruption—and corruption is never excusable—against the black legislators must be
viewed in relation to corruption elsewhere in the nation in Reconstruction days. If South Carolina legislators did treat themselves to
those famous gold spittoons and, allegedly, authorized contracts

[21] Vernon L. Wharton, *The Negro in Mississippi, 1865–1890* (New York:
Harper & Row, 1965), p. 194.

favorable to their personal financial interest, it should be remembered that these were the days of Boss Tweed when New York paid $11,000,000 for an unfinished courthouse for which favored suppliers furnished $4,000 chairs. If the black legislators of the South were incompetent, it was only in terms of comparative corruption.[22] Negro politicians were by no means all corrupt and there is evidence in some of the anticorruption proceedings that otherwise unobjectionable activities were seized on as an opportunity to discredit and drive black leaders, such as Robert Smalls of South Carolina, from public office. The allegation that the black man in politics during Reconstruction was unfit and corrupt to the point of threatening the American political system will not hold up. It was a myth; the Menacing Black Man was no threat at all.

But, in a larger sense, of course he was. The black man in politics during Reconstruction, briefly, had the rostrum. He was visible. He could speak out; he could demonstrate what he desired to be. In Reconstruction, he said he wanted what other men wanted. He wanted to be able to make choices about his future, he wanted to be with people he liked to be with (to have a family), and he wanted a farm of his own. Black people during Reconstruction struggled to become part of the electoral process not because they thought it would bring a second Day of Jubilee but because they saw it as the way to force white Americans to listen to them.

They worked to reconstruct America into one nation, but they were not allowed to succeed. Reconstruction was abandoned and the country, so recently disunited by Civil War, was left, in Ralph Ellison's phrase, "consciously divided" on racial lines.[23] Embarrassed by the disunity, we hide the dividing of equal men one from

---

[22] John Hope Franklin, *Reconstruction after the Civil War* (Chicago: University of Chicago Press, 1961), pp. 146–147.

[23] Ralph Ellison, Introduction to Stephen Crane, *The Red Badge of Courage* (New York: Dell, 1960), p. 14.

another under myths of Negro inferiority and savagery. Race can separate us; it does not have to, but at the close of Reconstruction it did. By force in Mississippi and with mocking and frightened prose from Maine, black people were forced to live in a second and shadowed land. America said no to the equality that black Americans and some white Americans, as well, wanted and worked to achieve.

The Boycott Movement against Jim Crow Streetcars in the South, 1900-1906*

AUGUST MEIER AND ELLIOTT RUDWICK

THE PRELUDE to the civil rights revolution of the mid-twentieth century was the dramatic eighteen-month bus boycott in Montgomery, Alabama, led by Martin Luther King, Jr. Unknown at the time was the fact that Montgomery had witnessed a two-year boycott by its Negro citizens over a half century before, when the city council enacted a trolley-car segregation bill. Like the bus boycott

* Reprinted with minor modifications as published in *The Journal of American History*, 55 (March, 1969), 756–775, with permission of the publishers and authors.

of 1955–1956, the streetcar boycott of 1900–1902 was part of a larger regional Negro protest against Jim Crow urban transit. The boycotts in Montgomery, Birmingham, and Tallahassee during the late 1950's had their counterparts in more than twenty-five Southern cities between 1900 and 1906. This earlier, forgotten movement was especially remarkable, for, unlike the Montgomery boycott that occurred in a period of rising Negro militance and increasing Northern sympathy for the Negroes' cause, the boycotts at the turn of the century came at a time when Southern white hostility and Northern white indifference were reaching their peak and when, as a result, a philosophy of accommodation had achieved ascendancy in Negro thought and action.

These protests arose in response to the Jim Crow streetcar laws passed at the height of the wave of segregation legislation enacted in Southern states two generations ago. Georgia passed the first such law in 1891,[1] but it required segregation only "as much as practicable"; thus, it left implementation to the erratic discretion of the traction companies. Then, beginning about 1900, a number of Southern cities passed municipal segregation ordinances. In that year, Atlanta,[2] Rome,[3] and Augusta[4] supplemented the state law with measures requiring segregation. Montgomery in 1900,[5] Jacksonville in 1901, Mobile in 1902, Columbia, South Carolina, and Houston and San Antonio, Texas, in 1903,[6] all passed such ordinances. Meanwhile, states had begun to enact Jim Crow streetcar laws applicable only in certain localities. Thus a Virginia law of 1902 required segregation in Alexandria and in Fairfax County.

---

[1] *Acts of Georgia*, 1891, pp. 157–158.

[2] Atlanta *Constitution*, February 6, 1900.

[3] New Orleans *Southwestern Christian Advocate*, July 5, 1900; Cleveland *Gazette*, July 7, 1900.

[4] Augusta *Chronicle*, June 5, 1900.

[5] Montgomery *Advertiser*, July 3, 10, 24, August 7, 1900.

[6] Jacksonville *Florida Times-Union and Citizen*, November 14, 1901; Mobile *Daily Register*, October 17, 1902; Columbia *State*, June 24, 1903; Houston *Daily Post*, September 29, 1903; San Antonio *Express*, October 13, 1903.

An act of Arkansas in 1903 applied only to cities "of the first class," and one in Tennessee of the same year only to counties of 150,000 or more. The latter statute, which affected only Memphis, was never enforced.[7]

The first state to pass a mandatory statewide statute was Louisiana in 1902. Mississippi followed in 1904; and in the same year Virginia authorized, but did not require, segregation in all cities. Tennessee and Florida required statewide segregation in 1905. The Florida law was declared unconstitutional, and the state did not enact another until 1909; but in the interim Pensacola and Jacksonville had passed municipal ordinances that the high court sustained.[8] In 1906, Virginia finally made Jim Crow streetcars a requirement in all its cities; and the following year Texas, Oklahoma, and North Carolina joined the list. In South Carolina and Alabama, city ordinances and streetcar company regulations provided a substitute for state action.[9]

Nearly everywhere, the streetcar companies opposed enactment of the Jim Crow laws by citing the expense and difficulty in enforcement and the fear of losing Negro customers. Often the companies were able to defeat such bills or postpone their enactment. Sometimes, however, faced with an aroused public opinion, the companies endorsed the Jim Crow regulation—even at the cost of reversing their earlier position.[10]

[7] *Acts of Virginia*, 1901–1902, pp. 639–640; *Acts of Arkansas*, 1903, pp. 178–179; *Acts of Tennessee*, 1903, p. 75; Memphis *Commercial-Appeal*, March 27, April 26, May 30, June 8, 1903; *Memphis Street Railway Co.* v. *State*, 110 Tenn. 602 (1903).

[8] *Acts of Louisiana*, 1902, pp. 89–90; *Laws of Mississippi*, 1904, pp. 140–141; *Virginia Laws*, extra session of 1902–3–4, pp. 990–992; *Acts of Tennessee*, 1905, pp. 321–322; *Acts of Florida*, 1905, pp. 99–100, and 1909, pp. 339–340. On the Pensacola and Jacksonville municipal ordinances, see note 70, this chapter.

[9] *Acts of Virginia*, 1906, pp. 92–94; *General Laws of Texas*, 1907, pp. 58–60; *Public Laws of North Carolina*, 1907, pp. 1238–1239; *Oklahoma Laws*, 1907–1908, pp. 201–204; Gilbert Thomas Stephenson, *Race Distinctions in American Law* (New York: D. Appleton and Company, 1910), p. 229.

[10] Savannah *Tribune*, September 23, 1899; Augusta *Chronicle*, May 15, 17,

Neither the streetcar segregation that emerged at the turn of the century nor the Negro boycotts against it was without precedent. There had been successful protests against Jim Crow horsecars during Reconstruction in Richmond, New Orleans, Charleston, and Louisville; but Savannah was evidently the only city of the period where a boycott was reported.[11] However, in every state and in many of the cities that passed segregation laws between 1891 and 1906, their enforcement precipitated Negro boycotts. At least three successful ones occurred in Georgia during the 1890's, when attempts were made to implement the law of 1891: Atlanta in 1892–1893,[12] Augusta in 1898,[13] and on the line from Savannah to the resort of Warsaw in 1899.[14] Thereafter, only five boycotts were even temporarily successful: Jacksonville in 1901, Montgomery and Mobile in 1902, and Jacksonville and Pensacola in 1905; and,

19, 20, 21, 1900; Richmond *Planet*, March 15, 1902, May 7, June 18, 1904; Richmond *Times-Dispatch*, April 17, 1904; Richmond *News-Leader*, May 9, 1904; Savannah *Morning News*, July 10, 1902, August 31, 1906.

[11] C. Vann Woodward, *The Strange Career of Jim Crow*, 2nd rev. ed. (New York: Oxford University Press, 1966), p. 27; Alrutheus A. Taylor, *The Negro in the Reconstruction of Virginia* (Washington, D.C.: The Association for the Study of Negro Life and History, 1926), pp. 52, 214; Roger A. Fischer, "A Pioneer Protest: The New Orleans Street-Car Controversy of 1867," *Journal of Negro History*, 53 (July, 1968), 219–233; Joel Williamson, *After Slavery: The Negro in South Carolina During Reconstruction, 1861–1877* (Chapel Hill: University of North Carolina Press, 1965), pp. 281–283; Marjorie M. Norris, "An Early Instance of Non-violence: The Louisville Demonstrations of 1870–1871," *Journal of Southern History*, 32 (November, 1966), 487–504; Savannah *Tribune*, August 27, October 22, 1892, September 16, 1899.

[12] Savannah *Tribune*, November 5, 1892; Booker T. Washington, "Taking Advantage of Our Disadvantages," African Methodist Episcopal Church *Review*, 10 (April, 1894), 480; Clarence A. Bacote, "The Negro in Georgia Politics, 1880–1908," Ph.D. dissertation, University of Chicago, 1955, p. 18.

[13] Augusta *Chronicle*, August 31, September 10, 13, 1898; Savannah *Tribune*, September 23, 1899.

[14] Savannah *Tribune*, September 16, 30, October 7, November 18, 25, December 2, 9, 1899; Savannah *Morning News*, September 10, 11, 1899; Augusta *Chronicle*, September 13, 1899.

of these, the victory in the two Florida protests of 1905 was achieved by court action rather than by the boycott itself. Boycotts have been identified in the following cities: Atlanta[15] and Rome,[16] Georgia, 1900; Augusta, Georgia, 1900–1903;[17] Montgomery, Alabama, 1900–1902;[18] Jacksonville, Florida, 1901;[19] Mobile, Alabama, 1902;[20] New Orleans [21] and Shreveport,[22] Louisiana, 1902–1903; Little Rock, Arkansas,[23] and Columbia, South Carolina,[24] 1903; Houston, Texas 1903–1905;[25] Vicksburg and Natchez,

---

15 Washington *Colored American*, March 17, November 10, 1900; Atlanta *Age*, n.d., quoted in Richmond *Planet*, April 7, 1900; Savannah *Tribune*, September 15, December 8, 1900; New York *Age*, July 5, 1900, in Hampton Institute Clipping Collection (Hampton Institute). Whether because of the vagueness of the ordinance or the pressure of the Negro boycott, until 1906 the Atlanta streetcars exhibited a flexible system of segregation, with mixed smoking sections at the back of the cars and some Negroes sitting with whites in the middle part. Agitation in 1906 led the company to institute a rigid system of segregation (Charles Crowe, "Racial Violence and Social Reform—Origins of the Atlanta Riot of 1906," *Journal of Negro History*, 53 [July, 1968], 245–246).

16 New Orleans *Southwestern Christian Advocate*, July 5, 1900.

17 Augusta *Chronicle*, May 21, 1900; Washington, D.C., *Colored American*, November 10, 1900; Columbia *State*, June 28, 1903.

18 Atlanta *Constitution*, August 16, September 20, 1900; Montgomery *Advertiser*, August 18, 1900; Cleveland *Gazette*, March 16, 1901; New Orleans *Southwestern Christian Advocate*, June 12, 1902; and Mobile *Weekly Press*, quoted in *Christian Advocate*, September 4, 1902.

19 Jacksonville *Florida Times-Union and Citizen*, November 11, 1901; Savannah *Tribune*, November 16, 1901; New Orleans *Southwestern Christian Advocate*, January 30, 1902.

20 Mobile *Daily Register*, November 4, 5, 11, December 2, 1902.

21 New Orleans *Times-Democrat*, November 4, 6, 9, December 4, 1902; New Orleans *Southwestern Christian Advocate*, November 6, 1902, March 26, April 23, June 12, December 3, 24, 1903; New Orleans *Daily Picayune*, November 4, 5, 9, 1902.

22 New Orleans *Southwestern Christian Advocate*, December 3, 1903.

23 Little Rock *Daily Arkansas Democrat*, June 2, 1903; Little Rock *Arkansas Gazette*, May 28, 1903.

24 Columbia *State*, June 28, 29, 1903.

25 Houston *Daily Post*, November 1, 2, 3, 23, 1903, March 8, 15, June 3, 1904; Charleston *News and Courier*, July 4, 1905; African Methodist Episcopal Church *Review*, 20 (April, 1904), 409.

Mississippi, 1904;[26] San Antonio, Texas,[27] and Richmond, Virginia,[28] 1904–1905; Memphis,[29] Chattanooga,[30] and Knoxville,[31] Tennessee, and Pensacola[32] and Jacksonville,[33] Florida, 1905; Nashville,[34] Tennessee, 1905–1906; Danville, Lynchburg, Portsmouth, and Norfolk, Virginia, 1906;[35] Newport News, Virginia,[36] and Savanna, Georgia,[37] 1906–1907.

This listing is probably an underenumeration, for there are serious lacunae in the surviving evidence.[38] The limitations of the

[26] Vicksburg *Daily Herald*, June 2, 5, 1904; Vicksburg *Light*, July 4, 1904, quoted in St. Louis *Palladium*, July 30, 1904; Natchez *Daily Democrat*, August 23, 25, 1904.

[27] San Antonio *Express*, March 16, 17, 20, June 16, 1904; Kansas City (Mo.) *Rising Son*, May 20, 1904; Charleston *News and Courier*, July 4, 1905.

[28] Richmond *News-Leader*, April 20, May 20, 1904; Richmond *Times-Dispatch*, April 21, 1904; Richmond *Planet*, April 23, 30, May 7, June 4, July 23, August 20, October 15, 1904, June 10, 1905; Baltimore *Afro-American Ledger*, June 11, 18, 1904; James H. Brewer, "The War against Jim Crow in the Land of Goshen," *Negro History Bulletin*, 24 (December, 1960), 53–57.

[29] Nashville *American*, July 31, 1905; Cleveland *Gazette*, July 29, 1905.

[30] Chattanooga *Daily Times*, July 17, 25, 26, August 13, 1905; Memphis *Commercial-Appeal*, September 7, 1905.

[31] Knoxville *Journal and Tribune*, July 6, 7, 9, 1905.

[32] Pensacola *Journal*, May 7, 14, July 2, August 1, 2, 4, 1905.

[33] Richmond *Planet*, June 10, 1905; Jacksonville *Florida Times-Union*, July 1, 3, 24, 1905.

[34] Nashville *Banner*, July 6, August 1, September 22, October 17, 1905, March 16, 1906; "Fighting 'Jim-Crowism' in Nashville," *Literary Digest*, 31 (October 7, 1905), 474–475; Richmond *Planet*, August 12, 1905; Indianapolis *Freeman*, October 7, 1905.

[35] Danville *Register*, June 20, 1906; Lynchburg *News*, June 15, 1906; Norfolk *Ledger-Dispatch*, June 15, 26, 1906; Norfolk *Virginian-Pilot*, July 15, August 24, 29, 1906.

[36] Newport News *Daily Press*, June 15, 1906; New York *Age*, August 1, 1907.

[37] Savannah *Morning News*, September 14, 15, 17, 23, 1906, February 3, 1907; Savannah *Tribune*, September 15, 22, 29, 1906, January 12, March 9, 23, May 18, June 1, 1907.

[38] Since the boycotts were not illegal, court records are not helpful. The Booker T. Washington Papers contain a few references to boycotts. The W. E. B. Du Bois Papers contain nothing on the subject (interview with Herbert Aptheker, November 22, 1968). Inevitably, one is compelled to depend upon

sources notwithstanding, it is evident that the boycott movement
was extensive. Protests occurred in all the states of the former Con-
federacy. Most of the major cities in Georgia and every major city
in Virginia and Tennessee had one. As the Mobile *Daily Register*
observed in 1905: "In every city where it has been found advisable

---

contemporary newspapers. Local white papers had every reason to de-empha-
size—even ignore—the boycotts. Neither in Memphis nor in Atlanta did the
daily press even mention the ones in their own cities. And where the local
dailies reported the beginnings of a boycott, almost invariably the editors seem
to have decided, after a certain point, that continuing discussion was no longer
in the public interest. Unfortunately, of the cities in which the boycotts occurred, only for Richmond, Savannah, and New Orleans are there extant copies
of Negro newspapers. Since the Negro weeklies were marginal operations that
lacked an efficient national network of communication until the rise of the
Associated Negro Press in the 1920's, news of events in distant cities necessarily
came irregularly through correspondence and "exchanges." Yet these exchanges
and, more rarely, letters that travelers wrote to editors, provided helpful information about the boycotts in a number of cities. Moreover, the Richmond *Planet*
and the Savannah *Tribune* published unusually complete accounts of the respec-
tive boycotts in which their editors played prominent roles. Also, in a few cases,
most notably in Jacksonville and Pensacola, and—during the early part of the
boycotts—in Nashville, Richmond, and Savannah, the accounts in at least one
of the local white newspapers are remarkably full.

All non-Southern papers cited are Negro weeklies. In every case but three,
when a Negro paper unequivocally reported a boycott in a major city, corrobo-
rating evidence was found in Southern white newspapers and almost always in
the local dailies of the cities where the various boycotts occurred. The boycotts
in Atlanta and Rome, Georgia, and in Shreveport, Louisiana, were mentioned
in the Negro press but not in any white newspapers consulted. In the Rome and
Shreveport cases it was not possible to obtain copies of the local papers either
on microfilm or at the Library of Congress. Both the Atlanta and Memphis papers carried news of boycotts in other cities, but failed to report such protests
in their own.

This is a conservative enumeration. A boycott certainly occurred in Wilmington, North Carolina, but it has not been possible to ascertain its dates. (See references to it in Charlotte *Daily Observer*, April 3, 1907, and Raleigh *News and
Observer*, April 3, 1907.) There were hints in the Negro press of a boycott in
Macon in 1899 and in Austin in 1906 and suggestions in the white press of boycotts in Asheville, North Carolina, in 1907 and in Galveston in 1906. These
have not been included because of a lack of firm evidence.

to separate the races in the street cars the experience has been the same. The negroes . . . have invariably declared a boycott."[39]

Negro protests through mass meetings, petitions to city councils and legislatures, and even an occasional boycott, often began while the segregation bills were being considered. In Savannah, for example, in 1901 a bill before the city council was defeated by the overt opposition of the streetcar company and by the more covertly expressed "conservative feeling of the leading white citizens," whose aid the Negroes had marshalled. Five years later, however, sentiment for segregation was much stronger among whites, and the Savannah Electric Company's president reversed his position. A Negro mass meeting urged defeat of the bill. The mayor, however, termed this protest inflammatory; the city council refused even to hear the Negro delegation and enacted the ordinance unanimously. In San Antonio, where the city council did permit a Negro committee to speak, an ordinance was also passed unanimously. In Jacksonville, after the city council in 1901 had passed a bill over the articulated opposition of the Negro community and its two Negro councilmen, colored people angrily stayed off the cars in an attempt to pressure the mayor into vetoing the bill. This boycotting proved futile, as did a similar step by Pensacola Negroes four years later, when they tried to force the city's streetcar company to lobby against the Avery streetcar-segregation bill, then before the legislature.[40]

Negroes resented these laws as a humiliating disgrace. The Nashville *Clarion* editorially condemned this effort "to humiliate, degrade, and stigmatize the negro." Several Lynchburg Negroes circulated a call for a boycott and termed the law "a gratuitous

[39] Mobile *Daily Register*, May 17, 1905.

[40] Savannah *Morning News*, July 10, 1902, September 12, 13, 1906; Savannah *Tribune*, July 12, 1902, September 8, 1906; San Antonio *Express*, September 15, 29, October 13, 1903; Jacksonville *Florida Times-Union and Citizen*, October 2, November 6, 8, 9, 14, 1901; Pensacola *Journal*, May 7, 1905.

insult . . . to every one with a drop of Negro blood. . . . Let us touch to the quick the white man's pocket. 'Tis there his conscience often lies." In 1905, after the Avery bill had passed the Florida legislature, Jacksonville Negro ministers urged a boycott of this "unjust, barbaric and . . . cowardly measure . . . in order to retain our self-respect." As the Savannah *Tribune* said, "Do not trample on our pride by being 'jim crowed,' Walk!"[41]

For Negroes the new order was startling, even shocking. One report spoke of the "mingled disgust and bewilderment" among Memphis colored people arising from the "obloquy and shame" imposed after forty years of unrestricted travel.[42] To men like John Mitchell, Jr., editor of the Richmond *Planet*, former city councilman, president of the Mechanics Savings Bank, and grand chancellor of the Virginia Knights of Pythias, the whites who demanded streetcar segregation represented a new and different Richmond. Mitchell maintained that since the Civil War no act had aroused "a more bitter feeling of racial antagonism." He deplored the passing of the "traditional harmony" between the races, survivals of which still existed in such events as the recent funerals of an "old mammy" and a church sexton who were buried from the churches and homes of the white Richmond patricians they had long served.[43]

Beyond this desire to preserve a status quo that in retrospect appeared to belong to a golden age of "harmonious," if paternalistic, race relations, there was the fear of physical maltreatment at the hands of "poor white trash"—conductors and motormen. The *St. Luke Herald* of Richmond predicted that "the very dangerous [police] power placed in the hands of hot headed and domineering

[41] Nashville *Clarion*, n.d., quoted in "Fighting 'Jim-Crowism' in Nashville," 474; Lynchburg *News*, June 9, 1906; Jacksonville *Florida Times-Union*, July 26, 1905; Savannah *Tribune*, September 15, 1906.
[42] Cleveland *Gazette*, July 29, 1905.
[43] Richmond *Planet*, April 16, 1904.

young white men," already universally hated for their overbearing and insulting conduct, would "certainly provoke trouble."[44] Jacksonville Negroes also vigorously objected to the provision giving police power to conductors as "bound to bring about a strife and possibly bloodshed."[45] In fact, one of the reasons urged for boycotting was the belief that by keeping off the cars Negroes would avoid occasions for friction and disorder.[46]

Although in some cities the white press either ignored or attempted to minimize the extent of the boycott, generally, where the daily newspaper reported the protests, the editors commented upon the boycott's singular effectiveness. Universally the effect was startling to the white population. In Augusta, where the streetcar company instituted segregation on Sunday, May 20, 1900, about two weeks before the city council enacted its ordinance, the *Chronicle* reported: "It was noticeable that the negroes did not take to the cars as usual on Sunday. On about every fourth car passing one or two could be seen." The Mobile and New Orleans laws both went into effect early in November 1902. The Mobile *Daily Register* admitted that "Nearly all of them are walking." In New Orleans, with its vast distances, the boycott was necessarily less marked. But there were so many empty seats in the Negro compartment that the whites bitterly resented having to stand. Little Rock conductors observed that very few Negroes used the lines most patronized by the race, "less than five percent as compared with the usual 60 percent." The day after the boycott started in Columbia, a white paper reported that "the absence of negroes was noted by everyone." In San Antonio, their presence on the vehicles was pronounced "a rarity." The Savannah *Morning News* commented that the colored clergy had been most effective in organiz-

[44] Richmond *St. Luke Herald*, n.d., quoted in Washington, D.C., *Colored American*, April 16, 1904.

[45] Jacksonville *Florida Times-Union and Citizen*, November 6, 11, 1901.

[46] Savannah *Tribune*, September 15, 1906; Jacksonville *Florida Times-Union and Citizen*, November 8, 1901; Richmond *Times-Dispatch*, April 20, 1904.

ing the people. For example, the paper reported that Thomas
Gamble, secretary to the mayor, had given his Negro maid carfare
to carry his two heavy suitcases to City Hall. When she belatedly
arrived, soaked with perspiration, Gamble discovered that she had
walked to town because her minister had admonished everyone to
keep off the trolley cars.[47]

The colored weeklies proudly carried similar reports. The Atlanta *Age* declared "that you can stand on the streets all day and never
see a Negro riding . . . unless he is going to Decatur, Edgewood, or
the River."[48] A Negro visitor in Houston was surprised at "the
completeness" of the boycott,[49] while one in Montgomery, nine
months after the local Negroes began walking, marveled at this
"universal boycott."[50]

The boycotts were easily sustained in the early stages because
they were a natural reaction to the humiliation and fears associated
with riding the Jim Crow cars. However, informal pressures were
also used. In San Antonio, a few days after the movement began,
six Negroes were arrested for pulling a youth off a trolley car. In
Columbia, the few who rode "were 'guyed' when the cars passed
groups of negroes on the streets." In Savannah, those who opposed
the boycotts were publicly denounced at mass meetings as "dema-
gogues and hypocrites." The city's police quickly took to arresting
Negroes who stood on downtown street corners, heckled riders as
they got off, and urged those ready to board the trolleys to take a
hack instead.[51]

[47] Augusta *Chronicle*, May 21, 1900; Mobile *Daily Register*, November 4, 11,
1902; New Orleans *Times-Democrat*, November 4, 6, 1902, and New Orleans
Southwestern Christian Advocate, November 6, 1902; Little Rock *Arkansas
Gazette*, May 28, 1903; Columbia *State*, June 29, 1903; San Antonio *Express*,
March 16, 1904; Savannah *Morning News*, September 15, 1906.

[48] Atlanta *Age*, n.d., quoted in Richmond *Planet*, April 7, 1900.

[49] New Orleans *Southwestern Christian Advocate*, December 17, 1903.

[50] Cleveland *Gazette*, March 16, 1901.

[51] San Antonio *Express*, March 20, 1904; Columbia *State*, June 29, 1903;
Savannah *Morning News*, September 14, 16, 17, 23, October 1, 2, 1906.

The traction companies were undeniably hard hit. In April 1908, the president of the Savannah Electric Company informed the city council that the boycott had resulted in a 25 percent decline in business and had cost about $50,000. He estimated that in 1906, when the movement was at its height, the company's loss was over $32,000. The Houston Electric Company, about five months after the boycott began, decided that it was no longer possible to disguise the fact that the protest was "crippling" its receipts.[52]

In three cases, the companies temporarily capitulated to the protesters. Jacksonville city officials, undoubtedly acting at the request of the traction company, ceased enforcing their ordinance after a few months and quietly asked the Negro ministers to inform their congregations.[53] In Montgomery, after two years, the company was so hard hit that it simply suspended enforcement of the law.[54] The president of the Mobile Light and Railroad Company, in the face of the Negroes' financially ruinous action, decided to test the ordinance in the courts; and he directed employees to permit passengers to sit anywhere. A conductor was convicted in city court for doing this, and the company announced that it would appeal.[55] There was no further mention of the case, however. Apparently, in both Mobile and Montgomery, Jim Crow arrangements were quietly reinstated after a brief period.

In addition to walking, Negroes pressed private carriages, drays, and hacks into service. It is doubtful that the boycotts could have

---

[52] Savannah *Morning News*, April 29, 1908, and Savannah *Tribune*, May 2, 1908; Houston *Daily Post*, March 8, 1904; Henry H. Proctor to Booker T. Washington, April 18, 1900, Booker T. Washington Papers, Manuscript Division, Library of Congress (courtesy of Louis Harlan).

[53] New Orleans *Southwestern Christian Advocate*, January 30, 1902; Indianapolis *Freeman*, March 22, 1902.

[54] New Orleans *Southwestern Christian Advocate*, June 12, 1902; Mobile *Weekly Press*, n.d., quoted in *ibid.*, September 4, 1902; Cleveland *Gazette*, July 5, 1902.

[55] Mobile *Daily Register*, December 2, 12, 1902.

occurred at all except for the Negro hackmen and draymen, who in that period still dominated these two occupations in a number of Southern cities.[56] In Jacksonville[57] and Savannah,[58] and undoubtedly elsewhere, the hackmen reduced their fare for boycotters from twenty-five to ten cents. In Savannah, the authorities became so concerned that the police began to look for overworked horses and to arrest unlicensed hackmen.[59]

In Houston, Negro hackowners lowered the price to five cents.[60] A Negro visitor reported that the protesters had developed an informal transit system of passenger vans, wagons, and carriages.[61] As the boycott entered its eighth month in June 1904, a streetcar strike forced Houston whites to walk for a few days. The Houston *Post* noted the amusement of the boycotters and the advantage they had by virtue of their "crude omnibus lines."

[I]n some instances the whites were hurrahed good-naturedly by acquaintances among the blacks. One well known businessman tells this on himself: "I live away out in the South End and having neither a horse nor carriage was forced to foot it to town. A conveyance came along driven by a negro and I asked him for a lift. Looking at me and grinning, he said: 'Boss, Ise bliged ter fuse yer de favor. De city council won't let de white folks and de black folks ride together, and I ain't got my compartmint sign up yit,' and with that he drove on." The negroes seemed to enjoy the predicament of the whites hugely, and along toward noon many of their conveyances could be seen driving about the streets with a space in the rear some two feet in length

---

[56] The role of the Negroes in the transportation system of Southern cities in the late nineteenth century is illustrated by the fact that the drivers on the Savannah horsecars were Negroes until the system was electrified and white motormen were substituted in 1892 (Savannah *Tribune*, September 3, 1892).

[57] Jacksonville *Florida Times-Union*, July 25, 1905.

[58] Savannah *Morning News*, September 14, 1906; Savannah *Tribune*, September 22, 1906.

[59] Savannah *Morning News*, September 17, 18, 24, 1906.

[60] Houston *Daily Post*, November 1, 1903; African Methodist Episcopal Church *Review*, 20 (April, 1904), 409.

[61] New Orleans *Southwestern Christian Advocate*, December 17, 1903.

blocked off by a piece of cardboard bearing the legend, "For Whites Only."[62]

The step from these arrangements to actual transportation companies was not a long one, particularly in view of the trends in Negro thinking of the period. Because of deteriorating conditions, there had been a shift in emphasis from agitation and politics to economic advancement, self-help, and racial solidarity, often coupled with a philosophy of accommodation. The development of transportation companies, therefore, functioned in three ways: as a means of protesting against discrimination, as a fulfillment of the dream of creating substantial Negro businesses by an appeal to racial solidarity, and—hopefully—as a practical solution to the transportation problems faced by the masses of boycotting Negroes.

In several cities, Negroes talked about forming a transit company; and in Savannah, two were actually organized, though there is no evidence that either put vehicles on the streets.[63] Only the Virginia and Tennessee boycotts of 1905 and 1906 produced functioning transportation lines.[64] Portsmouth Negroes obtained a "double horse wagonette" that seated about thirty passengers and made regular trips. Inspired by this example, members of the race in Norfolk formed the Metropolitan Transfer Company, which placed a yellow herdic on the streets—the first of a fleet of eight scheduled to arrive. Soon afterward, however, the white daily newspaper noted that few Negroes were patronizing the vehicle, since by then most had returned to the streetcars.[65] In Chattanooga, where

---

[62] Houston *Daily Post*, June 3, 1904.

[63] Savannah *Tribune*, September 22, 29, October 27, November 3, 1906; Savannah *Morning News*, December 13, 1906.

[64] Contrary to a widely held view at the time, the most noted of the Negro transportation companies, the North Jacksonville Street Railway, was not really a Negro-owned enterprise, nor was it organized as part of the 1901 boycott. Actually, its founder was an accommodator who had opposed the boycott, and at all times most of the stock was owned by whites.

[65] Norfolk *Ledger-Dispatch*, July 26, 1906; Norfolk *Virginian-Pilot*, June 26, July 15, August 24, 29, 1906.

the boycott started July 5, 1905, some unnamed "enterprising negroes" formed a hack line by the end of the month. After creating a stock company, they leased three carriages that made a regular schedule between downtown and a Negro section known as Churchville. Apparently this line did well, for in late August it was reported that, with the boycott continuing in "full force" and with the colored hackmen having "more business than they can handle," some "well known negroes" of the city had applied for a charter for the Transfer Omnibus Motor Car Company. A week later, however, there was evidence of a crackdown on the hack line. Charging that the Negroes were "working old, wornout animals from early morning until late at night and are only half-feeding them," the county humane officer announced that he would prosecute the operators of the company.[66] While further evidence is lacking, it appears that harassment by the public authorities forced the Negro entrepreneurs out of business.

The most impressive attempt to develop a Negro-owned alternative to the Jim Crow trolley cars occurred in Nashville. There the boycott began July 5, and by the end of the summer the leaders formed the Union Transportation Company. Its incorporators were among the elite of Nashville's business and professional community: the president was Preston Taylor, an undertaker and the pastor of the Lea Avenue Christian Church; its treasurer was a Fisk University official, George W. Henderson; and its purchasing agent was the Reverend Richard Henry Boyd, general secretary of the National Baptist Publishing Board.[67] For the first few weeks, the company used horses and wagons. By September 21, $7,000 worth of stock had been sold, another $18,000 worth subscribed, and five motor buses purchased. The buses arrived on September 29, and during the day large numbers of race-proud Negroes eagerly inspected them. According to the Nashville *Banner*, "the

[66] Chattanooga *Daily Times*, July 26, 28, 1905; Nashville *American*, August 30, 1905; Memphis *Commercial-Appeal*, September 7, 1905.
[67] Nashville *Banner*, August 29, 1905; Indianapolis *Freeman*, October 7, 1905.

cars are on the steam wagonnette style, and have a large front seat
with two long seats running backward, band wagon style. They
have a capacity for fifteen persons."[68]

The line began operations early in October. For at least a brief
time, it invigorated the boycott, but the buses never fulfilled their
expectation. The few vehicles naturally kept infrequent schedules.
To remedy this problem, the company's inexperienced officers over-
paid for nine more buses. These lacked sufficient power for Nashville's hills. Arrangements for boosting power were made with the
local electric company, but either the results were unsatisfactory or
the company reneged on its promises; in any event, the bus operations were constantly hampered. Little improvement resulted from
a new generator installed at the National Baptist Publishing Board,
and battery trouble repeatedly incapacitated the vehicles. Passengers became tired of waiting and increasingly used the Jim Crow
streetcars. Two years later, W. E. B. Du Bois described this enterprise as one that cost its shareholders $20,000 for a few months of
service.[69]

Legal efforts proved as futile as the transportation companies
and, though not entirely eschewed, played a distinctly minor role.
In a few cities, Negroes seriously discussed going to court, but only
in Florida did they actually undertake a legal attack. This litigation
was directed by city councilman and attorney J. Douglas Wetmore,
who twice carried test cases to the state supreme court. Arguing
that the state law of 1905 was "vague and uncertain," that it violated the equal protection clause of the Fourteenth Amendment,
and even that it discriminated among classes of Negroes by providing that Negro nurses accompanying whites could sit in the white
section, Wetmore persuaded the court to hold the law unconstitutional. The judges did so, however, on the narrow ground that to

[68] Chattanooga *Daily Times*, September 18, 1905; "Fighting 'Jim-Crowism'
in Nashville," 475; Nashville *Banner*, September 22, 30, 1905.

[69] Nashville *Banner*, October 17, 1905, March 16, 1906; W. E. B. Du Bois, ed.,
Economic Co-operation among Negro Americans (Atlanta, 1907), p. 164.

allow Negro servants to sit in the white section was class legislation. Negro jubilation over the victory and the temporary end of segregation was short-lived. Jacksonville and Pensacola authorities quickly passed municipal ordinances. This time there was no general boycott. Negroes in both cities again resorted to the courts, but early in 1906 the high court upheld both city laws.[70]

The boycott leaders, where they can be identified, were uniformly an elite group that consisted of prominent business and professional men, with at times a sprinkling of federal employees or a rare politician. Jacksonville, Savannah, Nashville, and Richmond provide the most complete information. In Savannah, the leadership included the outstanding Baptist and African Methodist Episcopal ministers, two physicians, an attorney, an undertaker, a prosperous barber with white patronage, and an insurance executive. The pattern in Jacksonville was similar, except that it was unique in including the city's two Negro councilmen. In Nashville, the prime movers were the Reverend E. W. D. Isaac, editor of the *Nashville Clarion* and the *National Baptist Union*, and the Reverend R. H. Boyd, president of the One Cent Savings Bank, as well as secretary of the Baptist Publishing Board. Supporting them were prominent citizens like J. C. Napier, former city councilman, cashier of the One Cent Savings Bank and later register of the treasury under William Howard Taft; Bishop Evans Tyree of the African Methodist Episcopal Church; the Reverend William D. Chapelle, secretary-treasurer of the African Methodist Episcopal Sunday School Union; and professors at Meharry Medical School and Fisk University. In Richmond, the most dynamic force behind the movement was John Mitchell, Jr. Working with him were two or three

---

70 Jacksonville *Florida Times-Union*, July 20, 21, 26, 29, 30, October 18, November 15, 25, December 6, 7, 8, 1905, February 7, 1906; Pensacola *Journal*, August 1, 2, 4, October 15, 17, November 22, 25, December 6, 1905, January 11, February 11, 1906; *Florida* vs. *Andrew Patterson*, 50 Fla. 127 (1905); *Andrew Patterson* vs. *Isham Taylor*, 51 Fla. 275 (1906); *L. B. Crooms* vs. *Fred Schad*, 51 Fla. 168 (1906).

professors at Virginia Union University, most notably J. R. L. Diggs, who was later president of Kentucky State College; Benjamin Jackson, grocer and former city councilman; and most important of all, the officials of the leading benefit societies and fraternal orders and their affiliated banks. Besides Mitchell himself, these included Maggie L. Walker, head of the Independent Order of St. Luke, and the Reverend W. P. Burrell, president of the Richmond Baptist Sunday School Union and general secretary of the United Order of True Reformers—the outstanding nonsecret mutual benefit order among Negroes of the period.[71]

Especially important was the role of the newspaper editors. Mitchell of the Richmond *Planet* and Sol Johnson of the Savannah *Tribune* clearly played leading parts in initiating and sustaining the boycott. W. A. Pledger of the Atlanta *Age* and Isaac of the Nashville *Clarion* evidently played comparable roles, although copies of their papers are not extant. The Chattanooga *Daily Times* denounced the Negro press of the city, especially the Chattanooga

[71] In the few other instances in which specific individuals are named in the press, they are of the same type: Dr. Charles Shelby and attorney J. T. Settle of Memphis; Dr. W. E. Atkins of Hampton, the most prominent Negro physician in Virginia; William H. Thorogood, a politician in Norfolk; and attorney I. L. Purcell of Pensacola.

Occupational information was gleaned from a variety of sources: the newspaper reports of the boycotts, city directories, and, for the major figures, from earlier research in the period. See August Meier, *Negro Thought in America, 1880–1915: Racial Ideologies in the Age of Booker T. Washington* (Ann Arbor: University of Michigan Press, 1963); Elliott Rudwick, *W. E. B. Du Bois: A Study in Minority Group Leadership* (Philadelphia: University of Pennsylvania Press, 1960). The role of the fraternal and mutual benefit orders in the development of Negro business is discussed in Abram L. Harris, *The Negro as Capitalist: A Study of Banking and Business among American Negroes* (Philadelphia: The American Academy of Political and Social Science, 1936), pp. 20, 21, 47–48; W. J. Trent, Jr., "Development of Negro Life Insurance Enterprise," master's thesis, University of Pennsylvania, 1932. On True Reformers and their importance, see especially W. P. Burrell, *Twenty-five Years History of the United Order of True Reformers* (Richmond: n.p., 1909); Harris, *Negro as Capitalist*, pp. 62–67; and an editorial by W. E. B. Du Bois in *Crisis*, 3 (November 1911), 9.

Blade, for stirring up "heresy" and disturbing racial harmony.[72] All six of the Richmond Negro newspapers supported the boycott there. In Augusta, W. J. White of the Georgia *Baptist* was nearly lynched for his denunciation of the Jim Crow law.[73]

The role of the ministers, in contrast, is a complex subject. The relationship of religion to Negro protest has always been paradoxical. The Negro church has played mainly an accommodating role, and its ministers have preached sermons about rewards in heaven for the meek on this earth. Yet Christian ideology has also served as a wellspring of protest from antislavery days down to Martin Luther King, Jr.[74] Ministers often represented the Negro community in dealings with whites, especially in the South. Such clergymen were influential among Negroes because they could obtain small favors from the white community. They were influential not because Negroes chose them, but because they were selected by prominent whites who utilized the clergy to control the Negro community.[75] A common dilemma was faced by the Reverend C. R. Dinkins, a minister in the Colored Methodist Episcopal Church and the principal leader of the boycott in Columbia, South Carolina. One third of the cost of his church had been contributed by white

[72] Chattanooga *Daily Times*, July 25, 1905.

[73] Augusta *Chronicle*, June 3, 1900; Washington *Bee*, June 9, 1900.

[74] On accommodating role of ministers, see especially Ralph J. Bunche, "Conceptions and Ideologies of the Negro Problem," unpublished memorandum prepared for the Carnegie-Myrdal Study of the Negro in America, 1940, pp. 135–136, 147, Schomburg Collection (Countee Cullen Branch, New York Public Library); Benjamin Elijah Mays and Joseph William Nicholson, *The Negro's Church* (New York: Institute of Social and Religious Research, 1933); Meier, *Negro Thought in America*, pp. 218–224. On the ambivalent relationship of religion to Negro protest, see Vincent Harding, "Religion and Resistance among Ante-Bellum Negroes, 1800–1860," paper presented at the Organization of American Historians convention, Chicago, 1967; Gary T. Marx, "Religion: Opiate or Inspiration of Civil Rights Militancy among Negroes?" *American Sociological Review*, 32 (February, 1967), 64–72.

[75] For numerous examples of this, see Ralph J. Bunche, "An Analysis of Negro Leadership," unpublished memorandum prepared for the Carnegie-Myrdal Study of the Negro in America, 1940, Schomburg Collection.

people of Columbia. He was a man "in whom we have much con-
fidence," said the Columbia *State* when it advised Negroes to drop
the boycott.[76]

Ironically, because of this pattern of using the ministers to influence the Negro community, Southern whites assumed that whatever happened there was the work of the "preachers." Clergymen
were, in fact, often pictured as the provocateurs of the boycotts. As
the Mobile *Register* said, wherever segregated streetcars had been
inaugurated, invariably the Negroes had initiated a boycott,
"backed by the exhortations of their religious leaders."[77]

It is true that often ministers were among the chief supporters
of the streetcar protests. They were prominent in Pensacola,
Jacksonville, and Savannah; they were the principal leaders in
Montgomery and Columbia; and elsewhere, as in Memphis and
Nashville, individual ministers were named as key figures. Yet the
individuals who stood out most prominently among the opponents
of the boycotts were certain African Methodist Episcopal and especially the Baptist ministers. The Natchez movement was in its
third month when it was drastically undermined by a religious
conference sponsored by the prominent African Methodist Episcopal minister, W. H. Jernagin. The delegates freely used the
streetcars in getting to and from the sessions. The Reverend T. O.
Fuller of Memphis, principal of the Howe Institute and later a
chronicler of Baptist church history, wrote a letter to the *Commercial-Appeal* and advised Negroes that "Law-abiding citizens can
do nothing else but respect" the provisions of the state law and
obey the conductors.[78] In Atlanta, African Methodist Episcopal
Bishop Henry M. Turner helped to break the boycott by ostenta-
tiously riding on the Jim Crow cars.[79] In Savannah, the ministers

[76] Columbia *State*, June 28, 29, 1903.

[77] Mobile *Daily Register*, May 17, 1905.

[78] Natchez *Daily Democrat*, August 23, 24, 25, 26, 27, 1904; Memphis
Commercial-Appeal, July 4, 1905.

[79] Bacote, "Negro in Georgia Politics," pp. 302–306; Savannah *Tribune*, Sep-

first actively supported the protest movement. But later, in the spring of 1907, the boycott began to break when influential men among the Baptist clergy and the faculty at Georgia Industrial College rode the streetcars.[80] In Richmond, the situation was the most extreme of all. There, even before the boycott began, an open split developed in the Negro leadership. The powerful Baptist Ministers Conference, consisting of the pastors of three-fourths of the Negro churches of Richmond,[81] opposed the movement and thereby seriously weakened it. United against the clergymen were the businessmen, the editors, the bankers, and the leaders of fraternal and insurance societies. Some of the most important individuals in this group were also Baptist ministers, but they did not serve churches and their identification was with the business community rather than with the religious leadership.[82] In Nashville, however, a comparable cleavage failed to develop. There, preacher-businessmen like R. H. Boyd were able to obtain support from important

---

tember 15, December 8, 1900; Atlanta *Independent*, January 23, February 6, 1904. Bishop Henry M. Turner was known as a militant colonizationist who denounced American racism in colorful phrases (see Edwin S. Redkey, "Bishop Turner's African Dream," *Journal of American History*, 54 [September, 1967], 271–290). Yet he was actually a highly complex personality, not easily classifiable as either a protester or an accommodator. Thus, he urged Negroes to vote for Southern white Democrats and engaged in political deals with Hoke Smith, while his colonization efforts were supported by the white supremacist senator from Alabama, John Tyler Morgan. Moreover, Negroes generally—even many Negro colonizationists—regarded the American Colonization Society, which Turner served as vice president, as dominated by racists and as hostile to the welfare of the race. Finally, it should be pointed out that, as in the case of the more recent Marcus Garvey and Black Muslim movements, separatist nationalism, even when associated with militant rhetoric, actually is a form of escape that avoids a confrontation with the white society and thus really functions as a form of accommodation.

    80 Savannah *Tribune*, May 16, 18, June 1, 1907.

    81 *Hill's Directory of Richmond*, 1904, pp. 1084–1085.

    82 Richmond *News-Leader*, April 9, 15, 20, 25, June 4, 1904; Richmond *Times-Dispatch*, April 20, 21, 1904; Richmond *St. Luke Herald*, n.d., quoted in Baltimore *Afro-American Ledger*, June 11, 1904; Richmond *Planet*, April 23, 1904, June 10, 1905.

clerics like Bishop Evans Tyree who were not businessmen. Thus, Boyd led a united community.

The elite leaders who headed the protest were known as impeccably respectable men rather than radicals or firebrands. Some, indeed, were close friends of the noted accommodator Booker T. Washington, whom contemporaries described as "conservative" in contrast to the "radical" minority of intellectuals that led the opposition to him and his philosophy of accommodation. Moreover, it should be emphasized that this widespread boycott movement occurred in an era when accommodation was in the ascendancy. One wonders, in fact, how this protest movement occurred at all, given the context of race relations in which it took place.

The trolley-car boycotts can best be described as a "conservative protest." First, this movement was conservative in the sense that it was seeking to preserve the status quo—to prevent a change from an older and well-established pattern. Second, it is also noteworthy that the boycotts avoided a direct confrontation with the laws, such as would have occurred if Negroes had insisted on sitting in the white section. There were instances of Negroes being arrested for occupying seats assigned to whites, but these were rare incidents and, except for the Florida test cases, not part of the organized protest movements.[83]

Third, the statements of the boycott leaders themselves were often remarkably moderate or "conservative." This was true even of the editors, who formed the most militant segment of the movements' spokesmen. The Nashville *Clarion* vigorously supported the boycotters, yet added: "Their protestations are mild and peaceable however. They exhibit no spirit of anarchy or revenge, neither do they make any threatening demonstrations."[84] Mitchell, one of the

---

[83] Memphis *Commercial-Appeal*, July 16, August 7, 1905; Chattanooga *Daily Times*, July 7, 1905; Richmond *News-Leader*, June 10, 1904. On Florida cases, see above.

[84] Nashville *Clarion*, n.d., quoted in "Fighting 'Jim-Crowism' in Nashville," p. 475.

most militant Southern editors, described a meeting called to plan the Richmond protest: "The discussion was conservative and it was the opinion of the body that the colored people should do all in their power to promote peace and avoid any clash or disorder on the streetcars." The Richmond *Times-Dispatch* took a similar view of Mitchell's activities. In reporting a mass rally, it stated: "There was no turbulence, no fierce denunciation and no fire-eating, as many had feared. On the contrary, conservatism was urged." The paper noted that Mitchell advised Negroes "to be conservative and law-abiding, but to walk." Sternly, he warned his listeners to refuse to be provoked into confrontations with conductors that would lead to a race riot: "Then you will see their guns, their Winchesters. But we don't want guns, we want peace, and the way to keep it is to let the white people have their cars." Mitchell repeatedly urged Negroes who did board the streetcars to obey the law and sit in the rear; he emphatically declared, "Do not get on the streetcars to assert your rights."[85] Similarly, in Little Rock, boycotters were advised to "be obedient to the law. Let no one get on the cars and attempt to undo what the legislature of the great state of Arkansas has done. . . . Never mind about framing resolutions or arguing the merits or demerits of the affair with anyone. Simply stay off the cars." In Columbia, Dinkins told the press that the Negroes would do nothing intemperately and that they regretted hurting the Columbia Electric Street Railway Company, since its officials were among the Negroes' "safe and trusted friends." Dinkins justified the boycott because "there was no occasion for this ordinance. . . . Everything was going along pleasantly and preachers here have always avoided discussion of racial issues, preferring to try to inspire their congregations with faith in their own race and to encourage them to trust and to depend upon the southern white people."[86]

[85] Richmond *Planet*, April 16, 1904; Richmond *Times-Dispatch*, April 20, 1905; Richmond *Planet*, April 9, 1904.
[86] Shorter College, Arkansas, *Voice of the Twentieth Century*, n.d., quoted

Perhaps the most conservative of the protest leaders were those associated with the National Negro Business League, which Washington had founded in 1900. Indeed, Washington organized the overwhelming majority of leading Negro clergymen and businessmen into what was widely recognized and publicly labeled as a "conservative" clique. Boyd, president of the Nashville Business League, in a letter to the evening newspaper, pointed out that it was at the request of traction officials that Negro leaders had decided not to protest against the bill in the state legislature. They had then vainly begged the company to attach separate trailers and hire colored fare collectors on the routes where there was the most Negro patronage. Since the company had "denied [them] even serious consideration," he continued, the colored people felt that actually it was the streetcars that had boycotted them. It was in view of this situation, Boyd concluded, that the Negroes of Nashville had decided this would be a good time for "stimulating the cause of the automobile as a common carrier." As this letter suggests, a secondary motivation behind Boyd's actions was the vision of Negro enterprise built on the Negro market, of Negro "captains of industry," to use Washington's phrase. Men like Boyd may have been as much interested in the possibility of business enterprise as in protesting discrimination. As he said at the meeting of the National Negro Business League in 1903: "These discriminations are only blessings in disguise. They stimulate and encourage rather than cower and humiliate the true, ambitious, self-determined Negro."[87]

Another leading Nashville businessman who backed the boycott and the bus company and who, like Boyd, was given to accommodating utterances was J. C. Napier. He was a man of whom Washington once said, "I have never heard Mr. Napier express a narrow

---

in Little Rock *Arkansas Democrat*, June 23, 1903; Columbia *State*, June 28, 1903.

[87] Nashville *Banner*, September 27, 1905; *Report of the Fourth Annual Convention of the National Negro Business League* (Wilberforce, Ohio, 1903), p. 24.

or bitter thought toward the white race." The two men were so close that Washington once offered Napier the presidency of the National Negro Business League.[88] In Richmond, also, prominent League people were active in the boycott movement. Attorney Giles Jackson, secretary of the Virginia League, proved to be an exception when he sided with the Baptist ministers who opposed the boycott. But others, most notably Dr. R. E. Jones, president of the Richmond League, were the movement's ardent advocates.[89]

Although Washington did not personally involve himself with the streetcar boycotts, he had publicly approved the first one in Atlanta in 1892–1893.[90] In contrast, it is interesting to note that the anti-Washington "radical" Niagara Movement, founded by Du Bois when the boycotts were at their height, paid no attention to them and failed to recommend this type of protest, even though two of its prominent members—J. R. L. Diggs of Richmond and the Reverend J. Milton Waldron of Jacksonville—were connected with the boycotts in their home cities. Indeed, the only public reference to the boycotts that came from the prolific pen of Du Bois concerned the transportation companies, which he discussed as exemplifying business enterprise rather than protest.[91]

Clearly, then, the streetcar protests were almost entirely led by conservative business and professional men. Their weapon was the boycott, a multifaceted response to oppression that protested and yet avoided confrontation with the discriminating whites. As the social psychologist Thomas F. Pettigrew has written, boycotts as a

[88] Booker T. Washington, *My Larger Education, Being Chapters from My Experience* (New York: Doubleday, Page and Company, 1911), p. 65; Washington to J. C. Napier, July 7, 1903, Washington Papers.

[89] Richmond *News-Leader*, April 15, 1904. See also W. E. Mollison of Vicksburg in Memphis *Scimitar*, September 9, 1904, clipping in Washington Papers (courtesy of Louis Harlan).

[90] Washington, "Taking Advantage of Our Disadvantages," p. 480.

[91] Du Bois, *Economic Co-Operation among Negro Americans*, pp. 164–165. The Niagara Movement was steeped in the tradition of middle-class reform tactics and failed to see the boycott as a strategy for social reform.

protest tactic have "the distinct psychological advantage" of appeal-
ing to "three major types of responses human beings can make
to oppression. . . . Such campaigns move toward the oppressor by
seeking to achieve desegregation; they move against the oppressor
by encouraging group unity and aggressively upsetting the white-
controlled economy; and they move away from the oppressor by
requesting the participators merely to avoid the scene of conflict."[92]
By attacking and yet withdrawing, the boycotters—like the founders of the Negro churches a century before—were both protesting
against race prejudice and accommodating to it.

It should be emphasized that, although the boycott was a tactic
adopted by many conservative leaders, partly because it avoided
confrontation and overt racial friction, it was, nevertheless, a genuine protest weapon. It was so considered by the whites and by
those accommodating ministers who opposed its use. But as the least
aggressive kind of protest, the least militant variety of what today
is called nonviolent direct action, it fitted the conservatism of Negro
leaders in Southern cities during a period of accommodation. Even
in such a time, the boycotts were a natural and spontaneous response, for they sought to preserve dignity in the face of a humiliating social change.

The streetcar boycotts varied considerably in length. The nature
of the evidence is such that in most instances it is not possible to
give a definite date for the conclusion of a boycott. After the first
few days or weeks, the white press usually ignored the movement.
Exchanges and other items from distant cities in the Negro weeklies
were not ordinarily dated; and, thus, even for the victories in
Jacksonville in 1901 and Montgomery in 1902, the Negro press
failed to note the precise date.[93]

[92] Thomas F. Pettigrew, *A Profile of the Negro American* (Princeton: Van
Nostrand, 1964), p. 200.
[93] In Jacksonville, where the white press gave unusually full coverage to the
protests, it carried no indication that the 1901 boycott had been successful until
four years later when, during the election campaign of 1905, the mayor's oppo-

In Savannah, where the evidence is the most complete, the boycott began September 13, 1906, and continued through the winter. As spring approached, the *Tribune* and the Chatham County Emancipation Association were urging Negroes not only to keep off the cars but also to refrain from patronizing the suburban Lincoln Amusement Park, owned by the transit company. Yet, as the *Morning News* observed a month earlier, "there has been a gradual tendency on the part of the negroes to resume riding on the cars." The last notice of a mass meeting published in the *Tribune* was for one scheduled for March 24, 1907. Actually, the boycott began to break down as important clerics and professors openly rode the streetcars. Some continued to walk, even though the majority slowly returned to the streetcars. In April 1908, the president of the streetcar company indicated that it was still suffering to some extent; he put the return of colored patrons at 80 percent. As late as the following September, a few, like Johnson, were still boycotting the cars. But by then even the *Tribune* editor conceded defeat.[94]

The boycotts ranged in length from a few weeks to as long as two or three years. The Mobile *Daily Register* generalized that it took "about two months" to convince Negroes that they might as well use the cars again.[95] Yet some clearly lasted a good deal longer. The Montgomery boycott was entering its third month when the Atlanta *Constitution* marveled at its "surprising persistency. . . . The company reports that the receipts of the line have fallen off fully 25%. All efforts heretofore made in Alabama to organize strikes among the negro miners . . . have proved unsuccessful and it has been believed that no considerable number of negroes could

---

nent charged that the mayor had failed to enforce the 1901 Jim Crow law. See *Florida Times-Union*, May 3, 16, 20, 30, June 6, 7, 1905.

[94] Savannah *Morning News*, September 14, 1906, February 3, 1907; Savannah *Tribune*, March 9, 16, 23, May 18, 1907, May 2, September 19, 1908.

[95] Mobile *Daily Register*, May 17, 1905.

be organized for any length of time . . . they have almost entirely refrained from riding."[96] The New Orleans and Nashville boycotts lasted at least eight months, the Atlanta boycott at least ten months, the Savannah boycott six to ten months, and the Newport News boycott fourteen months. The white press in San Antonio indicated the boycott there was going on three months after it began, and the daily paper in Houston reported the local boycott as still strong eight months after it started. A July 1905 report in the Charleston *News and Courier* indicated that both were still in existence—making their length fifteen months and twenty-two months respect-tively. And in June 1903, three years after the Augusta boycott began, the manager of the Columbia, South Carolina, traction com-pany reported that this movement was so effective that Negroes arriving on excursion trains from Augusta refused to ride the trol-ley cars even in Columbia.[97]

In some cities, like Atlanta, Memphis, Natchez, Richmond, and Savannah, leadership cleavages undoubtedly hastened the demise of the protests. But more than anything else, what undoubtedly caused their decline was a feeling of discouragement—a realistic pessimism—that must in time have come over the demonstrators as they saw that their withdrawal of patronage produced no re-sults. Some, like editors Johnson and Mitchell, might continue to walk, but gradually a sense of futility set in.

It is not surprising that, in the end, the boycott movements against Jim Crow trolleys failed in all of the cities where they were initiated. They occurred at a time when Southern racism was reaching its crest and when the white South had gained a respectful hearing in the North. With the Supreme Court endorsing the

[96] Atlanta *Constitution*, September 20, 1900; Cleveland *Gazette*, March 16, 1901.

[97] For New Orleans, see note 21; for Nashville, see note 34; for Atlanta, see note 15; for Newport News, see note 36; for Houston and San Antonio, see notes 25 and 27; for Augusta, see note 17.

separate-but-equal doctrine and with Negroes in most places virtually disfranchised, the boycotts were the only way of protesting realistically open to them. In retrospect, it is easy to see that their failure was inevitable. The remarkable thing is not that the boycotts failed, but that they happened in so many places and lasted as long as they often did.

The Myth of the Southern Box Office

A Factor in Racial Stereotyping in American Movies, 1920–1940

THOMAS R. CRIPPS

IT IS A TRUISM that Hollywood in its golden age between the two world wars was a mirror of American mores. A seldom-raised question is whether it was an accurate reflector of the American scene. In the realm of racial values and attitudes it might be demonstrated, in fact, that American motion pictures not only failed to mirror American Negro and white life, but, moreover, distorted it by basing production decisions on faulty information. In the twenty years between 1920 and 1940 the movie trade papers presumed the existence of a mythic, omnipotent Southern box office that reflected American racial values. Basing their decisions as to racial characterizations on flimsy and invalid data, the big corporations created a generation of servile Negroes who rarely stepped outside their stereotyped roles of butlers and maids. That the Hollywood Negro was based on erroneous assumptions about the ticket-buying patterns of white and Negro Americans may be seen by comparing the trade papers' own reports on the Southern box office with their articles on the eagerness with which blacks and whites bought tickets to musical, dramatic, vaudeville, and other forms of entertainment with prominent Negro themes and content. In effect, while Americans paid millions of dollars to see all-Negro revues, Eugene O'Neill plays like *The Emperor Jones*, and the "race" movies made for ghetto consumption, the trade papers continued to assure the producers that Americans would tolerate none but the most demeaning cinema roles for Negroes. A comparison of the mythic box office with the reality, and of the barren racial scene in Hollywood with the emerging rich tradition in theatre, is in order.

In the periods before and after those two decades Negroes enjoyed a modest amount of honest depiction in white men's movies. It was only during the middle period that numerous black movie companies survived on the fringes of the Hollywood scene, satisfying the ghetto market by making all-Negro "race" movies that attempted to treat black characterization with some integrity.

In the years before D. W. Griffith's *Birth of a Nation* in 1915, black characters reflected a wide range of behavior. Most movies then were one- and two-reel vignettes, newsreels, and documentaries. Some of them were horrid burlesques of Negro life, such as comic fish fries and watermelon-eating contests. But some newsreels recorded the Tenth Cavalry on the march and other images of competent black men.

Fiction films before 1915 revealed a number of black roles other than Uncle Tom and Sambo. One of the most visually exciting was a 1904 Biograph production, *A Bucket of Cream Ale*, in which an arrogant white customer berates a Negro waitress for sipping ale from his pitcher, whereupon she, rather than submit to indignity, pours the ale over the man's head.[1] There was never a wave of such movies, but, at the same time, there were enough films of the Negro boxer, Jack Johnson, pummeling white opponents to induce Congress to prohibit the interstate transport of boxing films.

A number of factors in the early period encouraged the depiction of a variety of black characters on the screen. Negroes were new upon the urban scene and white Yankees had not yet typed them as rigidly as Southerners had. Movies were still cheap to produce and men could more easily take risks that might appeal to the polyethnic urban audiences. But most important, it was not until D. W. Griffith's technically brilliant *Birth of a Nation* in 1915 that audiences saw gathered together all of the facets of the stock Negro character: the humble darky, the faithful servant, the bad blacks in towns, and the corrupt legislators of Reconstruction. By comparison, Griffith's earlier movies, such as *The Battle, His Trust,* and *His Trust Fulfilled,* stressed Southern romanticism rather than the poisonous racism of Thomas Dixon, his collaborator on *Birth of a Nation.*[2]

During the quarter of a century after 1940 conditions again allowed Negroes to fare moderately well on the screen. *Stormy Weather* and *Cabin in the Sky* were two of Hollywood's occasional all-Negro musical efforts that were acceptable despite a few stereotyped roles. No matter that there were tinges of white paternalism, a string of wartime social democracy and antifascist movies did well. The so-called message movies of the postwar period intro-

[1] *A Bucket of Cream Ale* (American Mutoscope and Biograph Company, 1904), print in the Library of Congress.

[2] Thomas R. Cripps, "The Unformed Image: The Negro in the Movies before *Birth of a Nation,*" unpublished paper read before the Association for the Study of Negro Life and History, Greensboro, North Carolina, October, 1967. On Griffith and Dixon see Thomas R. Cripps, "The Reaction of the Negro to the Motion Picture *Birth of a Nation,*" *Historian,* 25, no. 3 (May, 1963), 344–346. See also Raymond Allen Cook, *Fire from the Flint: The Amazing Careers of Thomas Dixon* (Winston-Salem, N.C.: John F. Blair, 1968), chap. 7.

duced Negroes as a social problem and prepared the way for the prim and pious films of Harry Belafonte and Sidney Poitier. And since that time human dimensions have slowly crept into Negro characterizations in such movies as *Nothing But a Man* and Leroi Jones' *The Dutchman*.[3]

Growing black consciousness and direct action coupled with white awareness of the racial implications of the war against fascism created an atmosphere in which such films could be produced. Each new movie added to the optimism generated by military victory and made Southern white intransigence seem less monolithic than in the past.

By comparison, the period between the wars was a time of unremitting racism with blacks providing only comic background for white stories or straw men for a succession of Tarzans. Only a few fine Negro characterizations shone through the haze of white attitudes. A reviewer credited Daniel Haynes with an "outstanding" performance in the 1932 prison drama, *The Last Mile*; while another critic remembered Clarence Muse's role in MGM's 1935 *O'Shaughnessy's Boy* as "far more important than the author probably intended." Other examples were Muse in First National's *Cabin in the Cotton* (1932) and Edgar Washington in William Wellman's egalitarian *Beggars of Life* (1928).[4]

The only consistently creditable sources of movies for Negro audiences were those made by a few independent whites and by blacks in the long-abandoned studios "back east." Oscar Micheaux and other black directors, and occasionally a few whites, such as Dudley Murphy, produced films like *Body and Soul* (1924) with

---

[3] Thomas R. Cripps, "The Death of Rastus: The Negro in American Films since 1945," *Phylon*, 28, no. 3 (Fall, 1967), 267–275. *The Dutchman* was given simultaneous theatre and 16 mm release. See Walter Reade-Sterling press release, March 23, 1967, in the possession of the author.

[4] *Variety*, October, 1935, clipping (on Muse); August 16, 1932, p. 21 (on Haynes). Prints of *Beggars of Life* and *St. Louis Blues* are in the George Eastman House, Rochester, New York. For a white response to *Cabin in the Cotton*, see *Variety*, October 4, 1932, p. 19.

Paul Robeson, *Emperor Jones* (1933) also with Robeson, and *St. Louis Blues* (1928) with Bessie Smith. This "black underground" even produced newsreels and documentaries through such companies as Leigh Whipper's Renaissance News Company and the All America News Company. One of their best efforts was the Lincoln production of the *Unknown Soldier Speaks* in which a disembodied voice of "the unknown soldier" recounts the services of black troops in American wars.[5]

But for the most part during the 1920's and 1930's movie production gradually fell into white hands, less willing to risk departures from proven formulas. As the infant art of moviemaking became an industry, making profit became its *raison d'etre*. And at its vast social distance from the rest of America, the movie colony could depend only on box office receipts as an index of American taste.[6] Bankers, investors, and producers, by relying on such data, fell into patterns, cycles, and types of movies, all of which were designed to sell. In a short time, Hollywoodians came to ignore other kinds of information about audience response and uncritically accepted box office receipts as the sole criterion of success.[7]

[5] For a discussion of the "black underground" moviemakers, see Thomas R. Cripps, "Movies in the Ghetto, B. P. (Before Poitier)," *Negro Digest*, 18, no. 4 (February, 1969), 21–27, 45–48.

[6] For anthropological approaches to Hollywood isolation, see Hortense Powdermaker, *Hollywood: The Dream Factory; An Anthropologist Looks at the Movie-Makers* (Boston: Little, Brown and Company, 1950); Leo C. Rosten, *Hollywood: The Movie Colony; The Movie Makers* (New York: Harcourt, Brace and Company, 1941); Leo A. Handel, *Hollywood Looks at Its Audience: A Report of Film Audience Research* (Urbana: University of Illinois Press, 1950). For an excellent brief summary of the question of the impact of films on their audiences, with special reference to the South, see Peter A. Soderbergh, "Hollywood and the South, 1930–1960," *Mississippi Quarterly*, 19, no. 1 (Winter, 1965–1966), 15–19.

[7] There are a number of corporate and institutional studies, the most reliable of which are Gertrude Jobes, *Motion Picture Empire* (Hamden, Conn.: Archon Books, 1966), and Bosley Crowther, *The Lion's Share: The Story of an Entertainment Empire* (New York: E. P. Dutton & Company, 1957).

Thus the convenient myth bloomed in the two decades of growing corporate rigidity—the myth that certain regional markets would refuse to patronize movies with racial themes and by so doing could alter the content and form of future films. The most pervasive of these mythical markets was in the American South because its presumed existence allowed Hollywoodians to explain away their own racial attitudes that had slowly been imported westward with each new generation of moviemakers. The Southern boxoffice became a monolithic creature that predetermined the substance of racial images on the screens of the entire nation. After all, the reasoning ran, if it *would not* sell in the South, it *might not* sell in the North. Besides, the profits made in the South, although smaller than those in other regions, could carry a movie "out of the red."

That the myth had little substance may be observed in the pages of *Variety*, "the bible of show business," and other trade papers. With unconscious irony *Variety* movie reviewers often predicted failure for movies with Negro themes while its Eastern reporters remarked on the quantity of "race" movies made for the nearly unnoticed ghetto market. At the same time, its writers also recorded the frequently well-attended Negro vaudeville, theatrical, and musical productions in most cities without noticing the implied box office potential of the urban ghettos.[8] Furthermore, a survey of the trade papers for the two decades reveals not only that the Southern box office was a weak predictor of financial success, but that many local Southern factors served to place the region near the bottom of all regional receipt totals. Only a few large Southern towns boasted comfortable theatres and even then the hot climate limited the length of the theatre season. Such outdoor amusements as picnics, baseball, and county fairs further depleted Southern grosses.

---

[8] Good runs of *Variety Showmen's Trade Review*, and the several mutations of *Motion Picture Herald* are in the Library of Congress and the Lincoln Center Dramatic Arts Research Collection of the New York Public Library.

Those movies that did reach the South were in danger of being ruined by capricious censors who snipped out not only scenes of miscegenation and "uppity" Negroes, but also many more bugbears of the rural Southern mind.

Generally, the movie trade journals, even while subscribing to the myth, held Southern grosses in such contempt that *Motion Picture Herald* reported no box office receipts south of the Ohio River. *Variety* used only five Southern cities as "keys," that is, samples of box office success. Of these, Baltimore, Washington, and Louisville represented the upper South. Only New Orleans and Birmingham were regularly reported for the deep South, with Memphis and Atlanta occasionally being reported.[9] Moreover, the best Southern cities compared unfavorably with the North. A good week's "take" in a single New York theatre, for example, frequently topped the grosses of an entire Southern town, and sometimes the grosses for the whole South fell short of the top one or two New York houses. In the week before Christmas, 1923, as a case in point, the best New Orleans house grossed $3,400 while the Capitol in New York announced a profit of $50,000 in that week. Several such big New York houses were capable of taking in over $100,000 in a week, but the best Birmingham house regularly fell below $1,000 for a week's take.[10]

Throughout the 1920's and 1930's *Variety* humorously singled out New Orleans' plight. The town was characterized in headlines as the "Champ Bad Picture Town," "Flopping Once More as Usual," where "Business is Bad and Sometimes Badder." Valentino's popular *Four Horsemen* set a record for low grosses there,

[9] Survey of *Motion Picture Herald* and *Variety* for the 1930's. By 1939 *Variety* used 26 "keys," of which only three, Baltimore, Washington, and Louisville, could be considered Southern.

[10] Sample stories on the Southern box office: *Variety*, October 27, 1922, p. 6; July 12, 1923, p. 21; July 19, 1923, p. 20; March 24, 1926, p. 29; March 31, 1926, p. 34; January 22, 1930, p. 14; June 11, 1930, p. 10; April 22, 1931, p. 8; June 2, 1931, p. 1 (for a Southern response).

while Pola Negri in *The Cheat* fell below $3,000 because, *Variety* concluded, she was Polish. Nearby, in Covington, Louisiana, in 1925, a theatre manager, desperate to fill seats, accepted empty beer bottles at the gate, earning only $23 and 1,812 beer bottles.[11]

Elsewhere in the South throughout the 1920's the story was the same. Each year brought a dreary round of excuses for low box office receipts: hot weather that closed the theatres from May through October, dog tracks, state fairs, free band concerts, and, later, night baseball. Even movies with Southern themes failed. *Dixiana* flopped in the South. Paul Whiteman as *King of Jazz* drew $100,000 in New York and slumped elsewhere. Even John Drinkwater's play about Robert E. Lee opened in Richmond, according to *Variety*, "Like a Wet Rag on a Foggy Day."[12] And in 1923, the fame of Thomas Dixon, scenarist for *Birth of a Nation*, could not save his *Mark of the Beast* from earning a disappointing $1,200 in New Orleans.

In the Depression years conditions predictably worsened. Baltimore cut prices and still attendance fell. The Strand in Birmingham went three straight weeks setting record lows and by the end of 1932 only one house in all of New Orleans was running in the black.[13] The Southern pictures continued to flop. In the South, *Mississippi*, a Universal W. C. Fields movie of 1934 that did well in ten towns from Providence to Cincinnati, fell 50 percent below

[11] For *Variety*'s characterizations of New Orleans see October 7, 1921, p. 31; February 25, 1925, p. 1 (on Covington); March 17, 1922, p. 47; April 7, 1922, p. 45; April 21, 1922, p. 45 (on Valentino); October 11, 1923, p. 23; December 20, 1923, p. 20 (for a comparison with New York); February 21, 1924, p. 16; October 8, 1924, p. 22; November 3, 1926, p. 6; February 16, 1927, p. 6.

[12] *Variety*, March 17, 1922, p. 47 (Lent); July 12, 1923, p. 23 (summer); November 3, 1926, p. 6 (dog tracks); February 7, 1933, p. 10 (Louis Armstrong at the Madrid Ballroom, Louisville); September 17, 1941, p. 13 (state fairs); May 2, 1928, p. 23 (floods, unemployment, automobiles); June 23, 1931, p. 1 (the "Whole South"). On Dixon's film and Drinkwater's play see *Variety*, September 3, 1930, p. 33, and for *King of Jazz*, June 11, 1930, p. 10.

[13] *Variety*, November 22, 1932, p. 53; December 6, 1932, p. 8; May 8, 1935, p. 24; July 25, 1933, p. 23.

the average of the Northern towns. Throughout the South exhibitors tried to save the day with double features. Near the end of the decade, Warner Brothers announced that it was dropping its Southern houses because of isolation and other "operating problems." *Variety* labeled Birmingham a "two bit" town where the natives must be paid in quarters—the apparent limit of their expenditure on a movie.[14]

Yet, during the entire period there was no indication that the consistently low box office receipts could be traced to the appearance of black actors or racial themes. Trade reviewers were invariably wrong in their predictions of Southern box office success. *Variety*, for example, was astonished that despite presumed Southern anti-Semitism, *The Cohens and the Kellys* did $11,000 in Baltimore in 1926. Even the success of big, expensive, "hard ticket" movies was unpredictable in the South. One such movie was Cecil B. DeMille's *Sign of the Cross*, which in New Orleans made less money than a horror movie-vaudeville double bill.[15] In short, movie exhibitors studying the Southern markets saw only inconsistency.

Similarly, there was no way to measure box office response to movies with Negro themes. Trade journals rarely tabulated the size of the black box office. In Washington, *Variety*'s correspondent totally excluded Negroes from his box office reports by using the euphemism "drawing population" to mean "white population." King Vidor's all-Negro movie, *Hallelujah!* did moderate business in New York, was above average in Washington, did well in New Orleans, and topped all other pictures during its week in Birmingham. Two years later *Trader Horn*, which featured a strong performance by a native East African, led all other films during its month in New Orleans. *Cabin in the Cotton*, a 1932 First National

[14] *Variety*, May 8, 1935, p. 24 (on *Mississippi*); October 5, 1927, p. 9 (on Warner Brothers); May 13, 1931, p. 7 (on Birmingham).

[15] *Variety*, March 26, 1926, p. 29 (*The Cohens and the Kellys*); January 24, 1933, p. 10 (the double bill consisted of *The Mummy* and Doc Rockwell).

exposé of the evils of sharecropping provided a powerful dramatic role for the black actor, Clarence Muse, yet its run in Louisville topped that of a comparable Northern market in New Haven. The same film was third from the top for its month in Birmingham.[16] Again, trade paper figures failed to substantiate the myth of a monolithic Southern box office that would not respond to Negro themes.

The pressbooks preserved by the Saenger Theatres of New Orleans and their successor, E. V. Richards, reveal that Southern reviewers did not consistently predict white response to Negro movies. Stepin Fetchit's broad stereotype of the lazy darky evoked many comments from critics ranging from no notice to praise for his nicely done characterization of a "lackadaisical rascal." One of his most unctuous roles, that in John Ford's *Steamboat 'Round the Bend*, drew no attention whatsoever from critics. Bill Robinson drew approval for his dancing in *The Little Colonel*, while being described as "of Harlem." By the 1940's most Negro players received a line or so of notice as "specialties," or "principals," and occasionally some special tribute as that for the Nicholas Brothers' "whirlwind of grace" in *Orchestra Wives*, or Paul Robeson's role in *Tales of Manhattan*. *Son of Fury, Beyond the Blue Horizon*, and other South Seas movies in which white women played Polynesians in interracial love affairs, apparently breaching the Southern racial ethic, also escaped critical attention.[17]

16 *Variety*, March 31, 1926, p. 6, recorded the "Estimated White Population" of the capital as 380,000; January 22, 1930, p. 14 (*Hallelujah!*); May 13, 1931, p. 60 (*Trader Horn*). Donald Kirkley, critic of the Baltimore *Sun*, thought that *Hallelujah!* arrived a year late as much because of its having no "big names" as its Negro theme: *Variety*, May 11, 1930, clipping. For useful, although biased, accounts of the Africans of *Trader Horn*, see Crowther, *The Lion's Share*, pp. 166–171, and Robert C. Cannom, *Van Dyke and the Mythical City: Hollywood* (Culver City: Murray & Gee, 1948), pp. 187–224. *Variety*, December 27, 1932, p. 10; January 24, 1933, p. 21 (on *Cabin in the Cotton*).

17 E. V. Richards Pressbooks, Drama Collection, The University of Texas at Austin.

The Southerners' own efforts at measuring audience response were often more serious than those of Hollywood. In a meeting at the Paramount-Richards Theatres' managers' school held in Bay St. Louis, Mississippi, in 1940, one of the sessions attempted to analyze the audience appeal of Eddie "Rochester" Anderson as an example of a regional favorite.[18]

Many other social and economic factors coalesced to prevent accurate inferences of racial tolerance from Southern box office returns. Even after air-conditioning made theatres more habitable, Southerners rarely went to movies during the warmer months. Frequent fires destroyed the old wooden houses when seasonal floods did not close them down. And by the 1930's fairs, carnivals, roller derbies, radio, and small-time vaudeville added to the woes of movie men. One of them complained in *Variety* that he would have to "turn the house into a tea room." Another felt that old rural habits made "show business in the South . . . just one big ache," because "the cities are made up of immigrants from the farm."[19]

Besides rural puritan habit, more purely economic pressures impeded accurate measurement of Southern box office responses. The Southern "gross national product" rarely reached boom proportions and often fluctuated with the vicissitudes of a one-crop system. Even when a headline optimistically reported "Happy Days in Dixie: Crops Up 25.1%," the writer reminded movie men that "when crops fail, the box office takes a licking."[20] Another local Southern economic quirk was the six-day week. While many

---

[18] Paramount-Richards Theatres, Inc., "Managers' Meeting: Elmwood Manor, Bay St. Louis, Mississippi, October 14–21, 1940," folder in Richards Collection, The University of Texas.

[19] *Variety*, May 2, 1928, p. 23 (flooding); November 20, 1935, p. 4 (one of many stories on fires, some of which were attributed to labor troubles); April 13, 1938, p. 24 (tornado); December 19, 1928, p. 15 (the "tea room"); February 23, 1932, p. 23 (on "immigrants").

[20] *Variety*, December 15, 1937, clipping. Even when cotton sold high, show business did not always share in the profits. Bill Sully, a touring actor, com-

Northern cities gathered some of their best gates on Sunday, Southern laws either kept theatres closed on Sundays or took inordinate percentages of the grosses for charity as the price of remaining open on the sabbath. Preachers contributed further to the exhibitors' costs by supporting high entertainment taxes and censors' fees.[21]

The various impediments were expensive fixed costs that ate deeply into profits. In one week thirteen Atlanta managers were fined fifty dollars each for breaking Sunday blue laws. One exhibitor complained that South Carolina's 10 percent amusement tax had closed more than half the state's theatres because it roughly equaled the normal net profit. States hoped to pay their censors' salaries by charging a fee of one or two dollars per thousand feet of film.[22]

Southern censorship proved to be, in its capriciousness and arbitrariness, another burden upon the exhibitors. In 1921 alone, for example, thirteen Middle Western states defeated censorship bills, while in the next ten years fifty-five Southern states and cities snipped film in outrageous ways. Atlanta's censor, for instance, was by custom merely the secretary to the duly appointed censor, yet rarely consulted her boss before ruining films with her scissors. The Memphis censor once proudly boasted that most of Texas, Arkansas, and Tennessee looked to her for moral guidance. Birmingham also depended upon the taste of one woman for moral enlightenment.[23]

---

plained of the many stranded shows in the South, explaining that despite a good crop "they are not parting with their money." Sully to "Al" [Fostelle], December 7, 1913, in Yale Theatre Collection.

[21] *Variety*, November 3, 1931, p. 7; April 25, 1933, p. 6; September 25, 1935, p. 7; November 20, 1935, p. 35; March 9, 1938 (Sunday laws); March 22, 1932, p. 21; March 8, 1923, p. 3 (Virginia's censor).

[22] *Variety*, February 23, 1932, p. 21; October 27, 1931, p. 21.

[23] See Ira Carmen, *Censorship and the Law* (Ann Arbor: University of Michigan Press, 1966), for a scholarly legal survey of state mores, and Murray Schumach, *The Face on the Cutting Room Floor* (New York: William Morrow and Company, 1964), for an informal treatment. *Variety*, December 27,

Moreover, Southern racial attitudes, because of segregation, prevented accurate measurement of the black box office. Many potential Negro customers declined to subject themselves to segregated
houses and those who did were not accurately counted. The Ku
Klux Klan provided, at best, an uneven barometer of reaction to
Negro movies because its members regularly harassed movies on
"moral grounds," or, as with *The White Sister*, because of Catholic
themes, or, because of Jewish themes, or because of legal suits over
the alleged infringement upon exclusive Klan rights to robes and
other symbols. If anything, exhibitors hesitated to use anti-Negro
films like *Birth of a Nation*, fearing that the Ku Klux Klan would
use the occasion as a recruiting device.[24] In short, for a variety of
reasons, movies did not make enough money in the South nor were
Southern moviegoing customs patterned enough to warrant influencing national tastes.

The myth of the Southern box office must have been a rational-
ization for what Hollywood producers would have created anyway.

1932, pp. 7, 26; June 10, 1921, p. 39. Except for *Birth of a Nation*, few films
had censorship troubles in the South solely because of their racial content. In
the North the NAACP conducted a long campaign against *Birth of a Nation*,
which may have prejudiced movie companies against films with Negro themes,
but, on the other hand, the NAACP executive committee minutes as early as
September 3, 1915, recorded their feeling that the film was "victorious everywhere." See NAACP records, Library of Congress. See also Cripps, "Reaction
of the Negro to the Motion Picture *Birth of a Nation*," pp. 360–362. During
the tenures of James Weldon Johnson and Walter White as executive secre-
taries, the NAACP drifted toward lobbying for better films rather than protesting older productions. Their manuscripts are in the Beinecke Library of Yale
University.

[24] *Variety*, March 4, 1919, p. 9; April 8, 1936, p. 30; March 12, 1941, p. 21;
January 28, 1942, p. 20; March 8, 1923, p. 3 (on segregation and public accommodations); January 14, 1924, p. 23; June 11, 1924, p. 22; December 22, 1922,
p. 39, and many other such news items. The influence of the Klan was problem-
atical in any case, as suggested by Thomas Dixon's repudiation of the modern
Klan as "unprincipled marauders." See Kenneth T. Jackson, *The Ku Klux Klan
in the Cities, 1915–1930* (New York: Oxford University Press, 1967), p. 131.

Several anthropologists and critics have noticed the unreal quality of Hollywood life emerging from its isolation from older, more complex urban centers. New York, the older capital of the cinema world in the days of Edison and Biograph, by comparison, seemed far more responsive to the needs of the many ethnic groups that composed its movie audiences.[25] Added to the factors of isolation was the rigidity of the giant corporate structures and their bankers, few of which would risk the untried. King Vidor, a proven director, waited years to do the all-Negro *Hallelujah!* John Krimsky, an independent producer of *Emperor Jones* with Paul Robeson, soon became lost in the Hollywood corporate structure. Those who rejected the system lost access to the tools of production. Kenneth Macpherson, for example, went to Switzerland in 1930 in order to use Paul Robeson in his experimental movie, *Borderline*. Sergei Eisenstein, the famous Soviet director, left Hollywood without ever beginning an intended biography of Toussaint L'Ouverture starring Robeson.[26]

[25] Hollis Alpert in Norman F. Cantor and Michael Worthman, *The History of Popular Culture since 1815* (New York: The Macmillan Company, 1968), pp. 222–224, argues that isolation affected responsiveness. In contrast, Albert R. McLean, *American Vaudeville as Ritual* ([Lexington]: University of Kentucky Press, 1965), chap. 1, holds that New York vaudeville was so socially responsive to its audience as to have provided a means of acculturating immigrants to American life.

[26] *Hallelujah!* pressbooks, New York Public Library. *Variety*, August 22, 1928, p. 7, reported that Vidor's film had been a pet project based on "his own observations in Texas and elsewhere of the everyday life of the Negro." A print of *Borderline* is in the George Eastman House, Rochester. For Macpherson's attitudes, see the all-Negro issue of *Closeup*, 5, no. 2 (August, 1929). Only one of Robeson's biographers took note of the film: Shirley Graham, *Paul Robeson: Citizen of the World* (New York: Julian Messner, 1940), p. 206. To most of the principals it was an experiment but to Robeson it was a test of his potential future in the cinema (correspondence between Cripps and Macpherson and Winifred Bryher, November, 1968). The producers of *Emperor Jones* derived their capital chiefly from the receipts from *Maedschen in Uniform*, a European import. Still, Marie Seton, *Paul Robeson* (London: Dennis Dobson, Ltd., 1958), pp. 70–71, thought that Jones's garish court had been a modification intended as a "sop" to the Southern box office.

Sometimes the timidity of producers was based not on racism but on their unwillingness to assume the role of social critic. Joe Pasternak, for example, believed that movies should entertain rather than comment on society. And since most whites saw Negroes only as social problems, black characters were easily excluded from the normal Hollywood productions. The gossip columnists also supported this view. Black people, resentful of the Uncle Tom stereotype depicted by James Baskette in Walt Disney's *Song of the South*, picketed the movie during its California premiere. Hedda Hopper's only comment on the demonstration was that "several Commie groups" were active in the movie capital.[27]

More important as an influence on Negro roles in movies was the pervasive racism in Hollywood. Even directors like King Vidor and W. S. Van Dyke, who had done sensitive pictures with Negro characters, retained vestigal racial prejudices. Many marketing executives, such as Y. Frank Freeman, S. A. Lynch, and Edward Kuykendall, either were Southerners or, like Sam Katz, had come to Hollywood from managing in the Southern theatre chains.[28]

Jack Warner remembered what was one of the most ironic tales of racial prejudice. It illustrated the potential of the Negro market for movies while revealing white blindness to it. In the silent era, pinched for funds, Warner rented a reel of negative to a Negro, explaining the reversed shading by telling him that the actors were black. The Negro billed the movie with a huge sign announcing

[27] Joe Pasternak, *Easy the Hard Way* (London: W. H. Allen, 1956), p. 11; Hedda Hopper, *From under My Hat* (New York: Doubleday & Company, 1952), pp. 285–286. For a discussion of movies as a "universal church" that minimized racial and ethnic differences as the price of assimilation see Parker Tyler, *Three Faces of Film* (New York: Thomas Yoseloff, 1960), pp. 105–114.

[28] *Hallelujah!* pressbooks; Cannom, *Van Dyke*, p. 137; Cecil B. DeMille, *Autobiography* (Englewood Cliffs, N.J.: Prentice-Hall, Inc., 1959), pp. 366–367 (on Freeman); Jesse Lasky, *I Blow My Own Horn* (New York: Doubleday & Company, Inc., 1957), p. 183 (on Katz); *Variety*, October 13, 1922, p. 46; March 15, 1923, p. 27 (on Lynch). Kuykendall attended E. V. Richards' Saenger Managers' School, Bay St. Louis, Mississippi, 1927. See Richards ephemera, The University of Texas at Austin.

"FIRST NEGRO MOVIE STARS." Warner remembered that "he had the box office jumping for three weeks." But the point of the story escaped its author, for Warner Brothers rarely made a movie with an eye to the Negro market revealed by the anecdote.[29]

As racial attitudes hardened, communication between the races became awkward, and racial stereotypes gradually replaced humane black characters in movie scripts. Los Angeles developed its own ghetto on Central Avenue. Dependent on the studios for work, its black folk rarely questioned racial policies. White men knew the ghetto only through the studio bootblacks, many of whom got movie roles because of their professional obsequiousness.[30] From the very beginning D. W. Griffith and his cameraman, Billy Bitzer, wrote marginal notes to each other using the term *nigger*. Even the popular "How-to-write-for-the-movies" books told young America the racial code. Some simply warned their readers to "stay away

[29] Jack Warner, *My First Hundred Years in Hollywood* (New York: Random House, 1964), pp. 62–63. Other racial anecdotes appear in Albert E. Smith, *Two Reels and a Crank* (New York: Doubleday & Company, Inc., 1952), p. 111; Robert Lewis Taylor, *W. C. Fields: His Follies and Fortunes* (New York: Doubleday & Company, Inc., 1949), p. 339; Bertha Westbrook Reid, *Wallace Reid: His Life Story* (New York: Sorg Publishing Company, 1924), pp. 10, 55–56.

[30] *Variety*, June, 1933, clipping, on the reluctance to sign Negroes who lacked a stereotyped drawl; *ibid.*, January 16, 1929, p. 7 analyzed Negro and white jobs acquired through Central Casting Corporation. Bishop W. J. Walls, "What about Amos 'n' Andy?" *Abbott's Monthly*, 1, no. 3 (December, 1930), 38–40, 72, complained of "jazzy, staccato, expression" and the "commercialization of primitive weaknesses," but black actors disagreed, for such expression was often their livelihood. See *Negro Actor*, 2, no. 11 (November 1, 1939), 1, in which Leigh Whipper wrote that "Hollywood Is a Swell Place." Charles S. Griffin, "Does the NAACP Speak for the Negro Actor?" *Negro Theatre Spotlight*, 1, no. 7 (January, 1955), 5, revealed a split in the black community over *St. Louis Woman*. Black actors wanted to work in it, while the NAACP thought it maligned the race because the central character was a Negro prostitute. Suggestive of the status relationships between the races in Hollywood, *Negro Achievements*, 9, no. 11 (November, 1952), 42, reported that Bette Davis "discovered" the Negro actor, Ernest Whitman, while he was working as a messenger on the Warner lot. The serials are all in the James Weldon Johnson Collection at Yale.

from censorable themes," while others taught how to describe racial and ethnic "types." One of the earliest of the handbooks offered as a model of "How to Write a Comedy" a story of a rabbit's foot featuring "a shiftless, worthless, fat negro" whose eventual good luck brings him quantities of chicken, pork chops, melons and "other things dear to a darky's heart."[31] Until Wallace Thurman came to Hollywood in the mid-1930's as a contract writer no black man sat in a position to rail against such stereotypes.

The absence of black opinion in Hollywood allowed whites to believe that their depiction of Negroes was accurate and desired by audiences. *Variety*, for example, reported in 1923 that Griffith "has long urged the idea . . . that this generation is ready for a new Uncle Tom," basing his conclusion on the success of his scared Negro character in *One Exciting Night*. Griffith erroneously believed that the film had done well in the South, while he ignored the fact that a shrewd detective in his own movie was an African from Scotland Yard. By the end of the decade, Harry Pollard realized Griffith's idea by making another in a long line of Uncle Toms. For Negroes its only virtue was that Charles Gilpin refused the title role because of Pollard's sentimental treatment of it and that James Lowe, another black actor, replaced him and gave the role an astonishing tone of militance.[32]

When, occasionally, movies captured some of the reality of the black world, executives learned the wrong lessons from the box office returns. A year after Pollard finished *Uncle Tom's Cabin*, King Vidor shot *Hallelujah!* on location in the South. By using an all-Negro cast he neatly caught the piety and enthusiasm of rural

[31] The Griffith and Bitzer Papers are in the Museum of Modern Art, New York. Associated Motion Picture Schools, *How to Write Motion Picture Plays* (Chicago, 1913), Lesson VII; Mervyn Leroy, *It Takes More Than Talent* (New York: Alfred Knopf, 1953), p. 75, warned his readers to eschew the "censorable" although he often ignored his own advice.

[32] Langston Hughes and Milton Meltzer, *Black Magic: A Pictorial History of the Negro in American Entertainment* (Englewood Cliffs, N.J.: Prentice-Hall, Inc., 1967), p. 300; *Variety*, May 30, 1923, p. 5.

religion in the black South while only occasionally lapsing into stereotyped gamblers and mammies. The film did well, even in New Orleans. In Memphis, Baltimore, and other Southern towns it ran without comment from local defenders of racial dogma. Yet the cycle of films that it stimulated consisted of the old stereotypes, such as Bill Robinson's vaudeville act in a string of Shirley Temple movies and Stepin Fetchit's mumbling, shuffling characterizations.[33]

The impact of Hollywood inflexibility may be seen in a cursory survey of the roles played by "the Hollywood Negro." As the black world grew more aggressive, demanding, and unified through the NAACP, the Universal Negro Improvement Association, the Urban League, and the "buy-where-you-work" campaigns, the Hollywood Negro grew more remote from the real world. From 1915 to 1920 half of the Negro roles reviewed in *Variety* were maids and butlers, and 74 percent of them were known in the credits by some demeaning first name, such as Napoleon or Flossie. In the decade of the 1920's the number of servile roles exceeded 80 percent of the total of Negro roles. In the more socially conscious 1930's such roles fell to 40 percent, but a new casting policy continued to restrict Negro roles. Performers like Cab Calloway and Lena Horne found it difficult to work even in musicals except "as themselves," that is, having no substantive part in the plot. Such billing accounted for nearly 15 percent of Negro roles. Added to these roles were the thousands of painted tribesmen who fell before the stout arm of Tarzan. Deviations from the norm came only after Tarzan's adventures carried him to New York or Guatemala.[34]

A few vignette black characterizations relieved the dreary trend. In addition to W. S. Van Dyke's *Trader Horn*, Vidor's *Hallelujah!*, and social commentaries of the calibre of *Cabin in the Cotton* and *Beggars of Life*, there were a number of prison films with Negro

---

[33] *Detroit Free Press*, March 17, 1929, clipping in *Hallelujah!* pressbook; *Variety*, January 22, 1930, p. 14, and February 19, 1930, p. 12.

[34] Derived from a survey of *Variety* by Mrs. Alma Taliaferro Cripps.

characters. Also Fritz Lang's *Fury* and other films criticized the
KKK. And in at least one film, Mervyn Leroy's *They Won't Forget*, the crime of lynching came into focus with Clinton Rosamond
giving a sensitive portrayal of a Negro victim.[35]

For the most part, however, between 1920 and 1940 Hollywood
remained ignorant of the black audience and its increasing dissat-
isfaction with discrimination. Never did the screen reveal this
part of Negro life. Civil rights protests and cases, NAACP opposition to revivals of *Birth of a Nation*, increased involvement of the
black clergy in such activities, and aggressive demonstrations and
lobbying against state laws allowing theatre segregation announced
the setting of a new black mood. Such famous individual Negroes
as Paul Robeson took up the cause by suing clubs and other facilities for racial indignities while whites joined in, as when Artie
Shaw canceled a Southern tour rather than fire his Negro trum-
peter.[36]

But the most remarkable blind spot of the moviemakers was
revealed by their own trade papers. They consistently reported
rising interest and creativity directed toward the race problem by
both Negroes and whites in other fields of entertainment. Powerful
dramas, exciting musical productions, racially integrated vaudeville and burlesque, and even expressions of white Southern concern with the Negro world appeared regularly, sometimes heralded
by Page One banner headlines.[37] Yet the ferment and excitement
were lost on the movie men.

[35] Prints of *They Won't Forget* and *Fury* are in the British Film Institute
in London.

[36] *Variety*, November 20, 1940, p. 2; February 21, 1919, p. 5; January 14,
1942, p. 44; July 1, 1942, p. 41; September 10, 1941, p. 1.

[37] All of the following were Page One stories, some with banner headline:
Variety, December 9, 1921 ("Plan Negro Grand Opera"); October 12, 1927
(reported the Broadway season as the best ever for Negroes); March 10, 1937
(more Broadway Negro nightclubs); April 28, 1919 (a feaure on Will Marion

A rage for Negro theatre began in the 1920's. As early as 1918 William Smith, a Philadelphia theatre manager, pointed out that the success of the Lafayette Theatre in Harlem should be taken as a demand for more black theatre. Such success extended to the white world, when musicals like Noble Sissle's and Eubie Blake's *Shuffle Along* came from the black scene to Broadway in 1921. *Shuffle Along* even triggered a movement for an all-black grand opera company. In the same year Charles Gilpin toured the South in *Emperor Jones* without incident.[38]

Negroes prospered in vaudeville and burlesque of the same period, with *Variety* reporting that "Negro Actors Are Flooding Burlesk." By 1924 Gus Hill of the Columbia Burlesk Wheel created six all-Negro and mixed-cast companies, and they played as far South as Baltimore before both white and black audiences. Vaudeville also had an all-black circuit consisting of fifteen full weeks of road companies in addition to three or four weeks of mixed-cast companies. In a single week in Chicago in 1933 there were all-Negro shows at four major houses, while at the Pekin the Mills Brothers appeared for an unprecedented seventh run. When a shortage of performers developed, boxers Jack Johnson and Battling Siki went on the circuit.[39]

Cook's Syncopated Band); April 23, 1920 (the expansion of Negro vaudeville); January 5, 1923, and August 16, 1923 (the decline of minstrel shows and "mammy" songs); February 7, 1933 (Grace Moore was dropped from the Palace card for refusing to share billing with a Negro); May 15, 1934 ("All-Colored Grand Opera for New York").

[38] *Variety*, November 29, 1918, p. 6; May 27, 1921, p. 28; December 9, 1921, p. 1; December 16, 1921, p. 1 (on Gilpin); August 2, 1925, p. 5 (on the recording industry). From 1920 onward almost every issue of the trade press reflected the rising interest in black entertainment.

[39] *Variety*, August 12, 1925, p. 8 (for headline); May 20, 1925, p. 30; March 31, 1937, p. 59; August 2, 1923, p. 31 (reported Baltimore burlesque men using the "colored show craze" as the occasion to desegregate their theatres); March 28, 1933, p. 2 (the Chicago scene, "a good town for colored attractions"); April

The demand for Negro musical comedy and vaudeville over-
flowed to Europe with almost every hit followed by a European
road company from *Shuffle Along* to Lew Leslie's *Blackbirds*,
which ran off and on in London for ten years. Another revue,
Dover to Dixie, starring Will Vodery and Florence Mills, "scored
a veritable triumph [and]. . . . Every number was violently en-
cored." Josephine Baker ranged from the Folies Bergère to clubs to
drama to such movies as Maurice DeKobra's *Siren of the Tropics*
and Marc Allegret's *Zou Zou* with Jean Gabin. French playwrights
followed the trend with such productions as Sacha Guitry's *Blanc
et Noir*, a drama that focused on an interracial triangle. Yet despite the rage for blackness, *Variety's* reviewer thought a French
drama, *The Black Ace*, "unsuitable for America . . . since it places
the negro in an unbiased light, almost idealizing him."[40]

Back in New York within a short time the musical was joined
by the drama. In 1925 *Variety* praised Paul Green's *No 'Count Boy*
especially for its acting, which seemed to come from "inspiration
and painstaking preparation" rather than the presumed natural
acting ability of Negroes. A year later Robeson opened in *Black
Boy*, thus adding to his growing reputation. In one season alone,
1927, there were eight black companies on Broadway, some of
them duplicated on the road. A year later, Wallace Thurman's
Harlem playbill included a glossary of ghetto patois for the edifica-
tion of the white audiences.[41]

28, 1922, p. 5, and September 13, 1923, p. 19 (on Johnson and Siki). Francis S.
Belcher, Jr., "The Place of the Negro in the Evolution of the American Theatre, 1767–1940," Ph.D. dissertation, Yale University, 1943, p. 133, estimated
that Negroes after World War I supported 328 vaudeville and 611 picture
houses.

[40] *Variety*, December 1, 1926, p. 4; June 14, 1923, p. 17; November 17, 1922,
p. 2; January 18, 1928, p. 23; January 29, 1935, p. 14; January 26, 1938, p. 57;
May 15, 1929, p. 3.

[41] John Selby, *Beyond Civil Rights [Karamu House]* (Cleveland: World Publishing Company, 1966); Edith J. R. Isaacs, *The Negro in the American Theatre* (New York: Theatre Arts, Inc., 1947); Loften Mitchell, *Black Drama: The*

As box office grosses rose in the 1920's radio joined the trend. Going beyond the Amos and Andy stereotyped roles, some stations sought black entertainment like Ethel Waters and her own radio revue. The Negro press in Chicago boasted that James Mitchell, playing "Wishbone" on his own show sponsored by Listerine, was the first Negro actor to appear on radio. A Mills Brothers advertisement proudly reported their grosses on a road trip, but closed by announcing their return to radio, which was awaited by "Millions of Listeners." By 1938 Moe Gale offered the networks an all-Negro show, *Harlem Hotel*, written by Juano Hernandez. Louis Armstrong also had a brief show sponsored by national advertisers. In Charlotte, whites jammed an unadvertised WBT radio show featuring the Mills Brothers. While in Memphis, WREC found in a survey that only one power source existed on Beale Street but that every house had a radio tapping the line for twenty-five cents per week.[42]

The boom, still unnoticed by Hollywood, brought changes in the ghetto. The black theatres were chronically short of film to show to their bulging houses. Black critics, such as Lester Walton of the *Amsterdam News* and Theophilus Lewis of the *Tatler*, felt secure enough with the new wave to demand better acting and production values from their black brothers in the theatre. Suggestive of increases in audience support in the Negro market, Chicago alone in one year built three new ghetto houses totaling eight thousand seats.[43]

Story of the American Negro in the Theatre (New York: Hawthorn Books, Inc., 1967) are useful surveys of black theatre. *Variety*, May 13, 1925, p. 25; September 29, 1926, p. 48; October 12, 1927, pp. 1, 42; February 27, 1928, p. 117; August 23, 1932, p. 37; January 3, 1933, pp. 88, 92.

[42] *Variety*, June, 1933 (clipping on Ethel Waters); January 31, 1933, p. 41; August 29, 1933, p. 64; February 2, 1938, p. 34; November, 1934, and July, 1938 (clippings).

[43] *Variety*, January 26, 1927, p. 1; March 2, 1927, p. 9; February 1, 1928, pp. 2, 15; April 3, 1929, p. 53.

By the decade of the 1930's, *Variety* headlines still blared such news as "Hectic Battle for Colored Attractions is Brewing in Philadelphia," and a regular column emerged, entitled "Extensive Colored Shows and Acts."[44] Negro orchestras began to enter the South, playing for both black and white audiences, further belying the Hollywood assumption that Southern whites would not pay to see black talent. Orchestra agents, such as Moe Gale, opened new night clubs in order to create even more dates for their strings of Negro performers. The market boomed to such a degree that Negro "tab shows" were used to prop up the grosses of weak white movies.[45]

Drama in the 1930's continued the Negro trend, yet with an edge of social protest. *Variety*, for example, praised George Sklar's *Stevedore* because "it gives the Negro his innings." Added to the movement was the Federal Theatre, for which Orson Welles produced a black *Macbeth* and an adaptation of Richard Wright's *Native Son*. The trend continued into the 1940's with the road show success of Katherine Dunham's dance troups and of *Porgy and Bess*. Success was marred only occasionally by squabbles over mixed Negro and white casts. And now and again a theatre owner would refuse to bill a show because of the presumed resentment of the local audience. *Variety* reported that Leonard McLaughlin would play Langston Hughes's *Mulatto* in his Washington house but not Baltimore because Washington was "teeming with cosmopolites and transients from the north and west, and is not considered a Dixie burg like Balto."[46]

[44] *Variety*, July 22, 1936, p. 56; September 15, 1933, p. 68.

[45] *Variety*, June 28, 1939 (clipping on Ellington); October 27, 1937, p. 49; June 22, 1938, p. 41; September 16, 1925, p. 43; April 17, 1934, p. 64 (advertisement for Negro bands); March 15, 1939, p. 43; December 4, 1940, p. 47 (Moe Gale); January 14, 1942, p. 11 (on boosting the gate by using Negro bands).

[46] *Variety*, April 24, 1934, p. 54 (Stevedore); April 22, 1936, p. 61; October 30, 1935, p. 66; October 8, 1941, p. 51; September 18, 1946, p. 52; May 25, 1938, p. 1; March 3, 1937, p. 1 (comparing Washington and Baltimore).

Yet, despite all of the activity in theatre, vaudeville, and night clubs, and the increasing evidence that white Southerners would pay at the box office to see black performers, Hollywood clung to its myths of the happy darky maids and butlers. Hollywood advertisements reflected the continuing racism, even for films that purported to improve the lot of Negroes, such as the copy for *Emperor Jones*, which read, "Your heart will beat with the tom-toms at this tragedy of a roaring buck from Harlem, who swapped a porter's cap for a tyrant's crown."[47]

The prejudices of Hollywood executives and of trade paper writers coincided, and, in the absence of accurate data to the contrary, racial bias and timidity forged the basis for substantive production, marketing, and reviewing judgments. The most flagrant case was that of Hal Roach Studios' *Our Gang* series, the oldest production unit on any Hollywood lot, and one with an egalitarian relationship among its child characters, yet the executives rejected a young black actor after his screen test for the role of "Farina," because he did not sound "Ethiopian" enough, that is, he lacked the requisite slurred speech pattern. Even Octavus Roy Cohen felt compelled to disclaim the possibility that the South might reject the movies made from his sycophantic Negro stories from the *Saturday Evening Post.*[48]

Trade paper reviewers either prophesied box office failure for black movies in the South or explained away every success as an aberration. While black movie theatres cried for more film, to the point of threatening to shorten their week, and white Southerners were paying to hear black bands, reviewers regarded as a breach of racial etiquette and a "hazardous experiment" Cab Calloway's playing a date in Dallas. Rarely would a movie with Negro roles bear the endorsement "sure fire for any audience." More than likely, its

[47] *Variety*, August 22, 1933, p. 17.
[48] *Variety*, October 27, 1926, p. 1; July 25, 1928, p. 1.

fate would match that of Joe Louis's fight films: predicted box office successes, "except of course in the south."[49] Of the successful *Imitation of Life, Variety* timidly warned that "its reception in the South, can of course, not be judged or guessed by a northerner. Exhibs below the Mason-Dixon will have to make their own decisions."[50] Even an innocuous musical comedy, Shirley Temple's and Bill Robinson's *The Little Colonel*, because of its Civil War theme, elicited the comment that "presumably expert advice had been obtained on that angle [the Civil War] in view of southern playdates."[51] When the Negro impact on the market was obvious, it was dismissed with some preposterous generalization, as in the case of United Artists' *Zombie*, which allegedly drew well in the ghetto because of the Negroes' belief in zombies.[52] The converse of this timidity was displayed in the excitement and ballyhoo generated by the movie of Stark Young's *So Red the Rose*, a box office disappointment. Its blatant evocation of the Southern mystique, although a financial failure, provided the opening shot in a romantic revival of the "Lost Cause," culminating in the enormous profits created by *Gone With the Wind*. No such cycle of Negro movies greeted the "surprising" success of *Imitation of Life*.[53]

Such slavish kowtowing before presumed regional tastes was always a Hollywood trait, but in the case of foreign markets and ethnic pressures, at least there was a stimulus in the form of protests registered by foreign governments or the outcries of special interest groups. The Mexican government, for example, barred the importation of films containing Mexican villains as surely as the Anti-Defamation League of B'Nai Brith protested the veiled anti-

49 *Variety*, August 1, 1928, p. 54; May 2, 1933 (clipping); May 28, 1941, p. 19.
50 *Variety*, November 27, 1934, p. 15.
51 *Variety*, March 27, 1935, p. 15.
52 *Variety*, August 9, 1932, p. 19.
53 *Variety*, December 4, 1934, p. 1; December 4, 1935, p. 7; November, 1935 (clipping).

Semitism in DeMille's *King of Kings.* The South African government was especially rigid in its censorship policy,[54] rejecting anything that could be construed as ridiculing the white race. Hollywood frequently responded with frantic mollifying gestures.

On the other hand, the movie industry's knowledge of the racial customs of the South was based on ephemeral archaic information. Even the most obvious evidence of public disenchantment with sentimental Southern minstrelsy, for example, seemed to escape the attention of the West Coast movie men. As early as 1915 *Billboard* regularly printed lists of minstrel acts who were "at liberty" and seeking work. By the beginning of the period between the wars, minstrel shows had died out in small provincial houses. The aging Duncan Sisters with their old-fashioned Topsy and Eva act suffered the barbs of *Variety*'s critic when they opened in Hollywood. And when Al Jolson's *Mammy* was released in 1930, *Variety* was quick to point out that it was not selling as early Jolson products had and urged families to see it as a dying glimpse of an earlier day. Yet the studios continued to grind out still later examples of the same genre.[55]

Thus, by the middle 1930's misinformation and timidity still characterized Hollywood efforts to deal with racial themes, as well as *Variety*'s attempts to interpret their success. For example, in its report on *Artists and Models, Variety* agreed strikingly with the racial attitudes of the Memphis censor. In the picture Martha Raye did a blackface dance routine with Louis Armstrong, and the reviewer complained that "while Miss Raye is under cork, this intermingling of the races isn't wise. . . . It may hurt her personally."[56] Even at the beginning of the liberal World War II era, Arthur Hornblow, Jr., of Paramount denied Eddie Anderson an opportuni-

[54] *Variety*, June 15, 1927, p. 1; January 11, 1928, p. 4; September 21, 1931, p. 21.
[55] *Billboard*, 27, no. 40 (October 2, 1915), 20, 43, 50; *Variety*, January 5, 1923, p. 1; February 19, 1930, p. 2; April 2, 1930, p. 19; October 28, 1942, p. 50.
[56] *Variety*, August 4, 1937, p. 18.

ty to do a film biography of Bert Williams on the grounds that "public reaction to the idea" would first have to be ascertained.[57]

Not until World War II did Hollywood eschew "the gutlessness exhibited in the past" by abandoning the policy of bending to the whims of foreign governments.[58] But no such change of attitude toward the Southern box office altered domestic movie products. While MGM in 1938 continued the production of *Idiot's Delight* despite Italian protests and *It Can't Happen Here* in the face of German resentment, and while Selznick-International pressed on with *Titanic* in spite of the objections of both the British government and the Cunard Line,[59] most executives still believed, with Joseph Schenk of Loew's, that the industry "doesn't mold the public; the public molds us."[60]

Finally, in 1942 a trade paper headlined a story: "Better Breaks for Negroes in Hollywood." And even then, after negotiations and dinner meetings between Darryl Zanuck and Walter Wanger of the film industry, the Republican presidential candidate, Wendell Willkie, and Walter White of the NAACP, most Negro roles remained peripheral except where they were treated as social problems.[61]

Meanwhile, throughout the twenty-year period, creativity and imagination came almost entirely out of the black underground cinema—the "race" movies. Based chiefly in New York, surviving on shoestring budgets and inadequate training and equipment, they successfully made movies for black audiences. As far back as 1915 Booker T. Washington, the NAACP, and a few white backers organized to produce *The Birth of a Race* as a counterirritant to *Birth of a Nation*. Along the way, most of the original participants aban-

[57] *Variety*, October, 1940 (clipping).
[58] *Variety*, January 7, 1942, p. 9.
[59] *Variety*, November 23, 1938, p. 1.
[60] *Variety*, October 1, 1941, p. 24.
[61] *Variety*, March 25, 1942, p. 1.

doned the project and it emerged as an artistic and financial failure, which nevertheless opened the way for future black films.[62]

During the 1920's several companies were organized by black entrepreneurs, occasionally with white backers. The Dunbar Company, the Colored Players Corporation, Leigh Whipper's Renaissance News Company, Roseland, and others turned out "race" films. They ranged from comic parodies of "white" themes, such as Ebony's *A Black Sherlock*, to Oscar Micheaux' 1924 melodrama, *Body and Soul* with Paul Robeson, which drew praise from the white trade papers.[63]

During the sound film era the black film companies produced a number of successful movies. The Lincoln Company's production of Bill Robinson's *Harlem is Heaven* was one of the best, but even weak films like Micheaux' first Negro talkie, *The Exile*, were often praised for some redeeming virtue, usually the good jazz on the sound track. Further growth and quality were thwarted by the Negro moviemakers' inability to penetrate the Hollywood distribution system or to gain consistent financial support from the big white companies. This segregation from the mainstream gave to the films a distinguishing mystique, but it also resulted in such uneven production values as the disparate acting styles that marred the films because of the necessity of throwing amateurs and professionals together. Sometimes the writers, attempting to create the illusion of major studio quality, imitated Hollywood stereotypes, causing Harlem audiences to laugh in the wrong places. Yet there was no source of movies to which the black world could turn other than the little coterie of independent producers grinding out their movies in abandoned Eastern studios.[64]

[62] Correspondence in Booker T. Washington Papers, Box 75, Library of Congress; scattered letters in Emmett Scott Papers, Morgan State College; boxes labeled *Birth of a Nation* in NAACP Records, Library of Congress.

[63] Cripps, "Movies in the Ghetto," pp. 24–27.

[64] *Ibid.*, pp. 27, 45–48.

Until the crude beginnings of the social "message movies" of the 1940's and 1950's, Hollywood failed to accommodate to Negro tastes. And, even then, the resulting change in Negro moviegoing habits served more to destroy the black companies than to place good black characterizations upon American movie screens.

But worse than the destruction of the black companies was the continuing caste mark of comic inferiority placed upon the black world by the "Hollywood Negro" of the preceding twenty years. In that period, because of its isolation from changes in American life, isolation from the black world, even on its own Central Avenue, and isolation from its own audience, Hollywood looked at the world through the prism of the mythical Southern box office. The prism was a distortion of American values that permitted the major film companies, their executives in marketing and production, and their performers to believe that the tastes and prejudices of the American South were at the core of their own decision-making processes. Most of all, it allowed them the luxury of creating the concommitant myth of their own innocence.

The "Organized Negro"

The National Association for the
Advancement of Colored People and Civil Rights

ROBERT L. ZANGRANDO

OVER THE PAST ONE HUNDRED YEARS, from the close of the Civil War to the present, from the end of slavery to the frustrating and embittering experiences of the black man in contemporary America, the status of the Negro probably reached its lowest and most depressed point in the early years of the twentieth century.

At the turn of the century the Negro lived in an American society that casually and unquestioningly accepted the concept of Negro inferiority. Social theorists seized upon and distorted Darwinian concepts to confirm what the white man already believed: that Americans of "old" stock, tracing their lineage to northern and western Europe, were superior to the "new" immigrants from other parts of the Old World, to Negroes and to brown- and yellow-skin colonial peoples.[1]

Beyond theory, in the realm of practice, white Americans worked vigorously to enforce these racist beliefs. Throughout the South and the border states, formal state-wide legislation and municipal ordinances set the Negro apart and deprived him of his full rights to participate in civic, political, economic, and social opportunities. In the North and West, patterns of discrimination were imposed, largely by practice but sometimes by statute. Overt and pervasive discrimination on the part of the public and its lawmakers was also accorded judicial sanction in a series of Supreme Court decisions highlighted by the Civil Rights Cases of 1883 and by *Plessy* v. *Ferguson* of 1896.[2] The dominant white majority showed no inclination for making the equal protection clause of the Fourteenth Amendment a working reality, and the high promise of freedom born of the Civil War and the early years of Reconstruction seemed irrevocably forfeited.

Moreover, a white society that could so totally and cavalierly reject the rights of nine million black citizens was able to employ forceful repression at will. Negroes were victimized in the race riots of 1898 in Wilmington, North Carolina, of 1900 in New York City, and of 1906 in Atlanta. These brutalities were repeated in the Springfield, Illinois, race riot of 1908, the East St. Louis, Illinois, riot of 1917, and the wanton destruction of Negro life and property

---

[1] For a discussion of racial attitudes in late nineteenth- and early twentieth-century America, see Oscar Handlin, *Race and Nationality in American Life* (Garden City, N.Y.: Doubleday and Company, 1957), chap. 5; August Meier, *Negro Thought in America, 1880–1915* (Ann Arbor: Ann Arbor Paperbacks, 1966), pp. 161–167; C. Vann Woodward, *The Strange Career of Jim Crow* (New York: Oxford University Press, 1960), chap. 2; I. A. Newby, *Jim Crow's Defense* (Baton Rouge: Louisiana State University Press, 1965), chap. 1; Claude H. Nolen, *The Negro's Image in the South* (Lexington: University of Kentucky Press, 1967), chap. 9.

[2] Supreme Court of the United States, 109 U.S. 3 (1883), and 163 U.S. 537 (1896).

in two dozen cities in 1919.[3] White lynchers acted with impunity; the number of reported lynchings of black men exceeded one hundred in nine out of the eleven years from 1891 through 1901, and seventy-six Negroes were lynched in that troubled year, 1919.[4]

In the face of such repression and brutality the American Negro was almost defenseless. Stripped of his political and civil rights, he had no ready means to effect redress; confronted with segregated, inferior educational facilities at all levels and with discriminatory employment opportunities, he lacked much of the broad knowledge and financial resources necessary to mobilize an effective attack upon racial injustices. What he desperately needed was a national organization sufficiently powerful to call into play the most concerned and alert interests within the black and white communities and marshal these talents and resources to achieve reform. This essential instrument was fashioned in 1909 with the founding of the National Association for the Advancement of Colored People.[5]

Negroes did not lack organizational experiences in the late nineteenth and early twentieth centuries. T. Thomas Fortune founded the Afro-American League in January of 1890, but its life was short and its impact slight; the same can be said for its successor, the Afro-American Council, organized in 1898.[6] The most prominent

[3] August Meier and Elliott Rudwick have discussed several of these riots in the political and social context in which they occurred, *From Plantation to Ghetto* (New York: Hill and Wang, 1966), pp. 161–170, 192–197; for a detailed discussion of the East St. Louis riot, see Elliott Rudwick, *Race Riot at East St. Louis, July 2, 1917* (Carbondale: Southern Illinois University Press, 1964); Arthur I. Waskow, *From Race Riot to Sit-In, 1919 and the 1960's* (Garden City, N.Y.: Doubleday and Company, 1966), has examined the extent and nature of mob action at the close of World War I.

[4] United States Bureau of the Census, *Historical Statistics of the United States, from Colonial Times to 1957* (Washington, D.C.: U.S. Government Printing Office, 1961), p. 218.

[5] The most satisfactory study of the founding and early years of the Association is Charles Flint Kellogg, *NAACP*, vol. 1 (Baltimore: The Johns Hopkins Press, 1967).

[6] August Meier has discussed both organizations in *Negro Thought in America*, pp. 128–130, 172–174.

Negro spokesman of the day, Booker T. Washington, seemed—
from his public statements on accommodation and his emphasis on
the Negro's need to develop economic self-help the better to play
an industrial and functional role in the New South[7]—more nearly
to reflect the depressed condition of the black man in America than
to represent a vital force for change. If William Monroe Trotter's
Boston *Guardian*[8] and W. E. B. Du Bois's *The Souls of Black Folk*
and his short-lived Niagara Movement[9] indicated a growing anger
among well-educated Negroes, it was also true that these efforts
were, of themselves, insufficient to generate the type of broad interracial reform that alone could allow the Negro to participate
meaningfully in American life.

Fortunately, a number of thoughtful, prominent white reformers
also recognized the need for interracial change. In January of 1908,
for example, Oswald Garrison Villard, president of the *New York
Evening Post*, wrote to Booker T. Washington to say:

> . . . the more I study the situation of the colored people the more I am
> convinced that what is needed now above anything else is a strong cen-
> tral defence committee, regularly incorporated and able to receive
> gifts and bequests for the furtherance of the welfare of the colored
> people by buying land, employing lawyers to take all cases of discrimi-
> nation into the court, to prosecute lynchers and offer rewards for their
> apprehension, to agitate for the restoration of civil rights where denied,

---

[7] See Washington's Address to the Cotton States and International Exposition,
on September 18, 1895, as an example of his public position. Booker T. Washington, *Up from Slavery* (New York: Doubleday, Page, and Co., 1909), pp.
218–225.

[8] For a treatment of Trotter as an outspoken critic of Booker T. Washington,
see Elliott Rudwick, *W. E. B. Du Bois: Propagandist of the Negro Protest* (New
York: Atheneum, 1968 reprinting), pp. 65–75.

[9] *Ibid.*, pp. 68–69, 94–120. See also Francis L. Broderick, *W. E. B. Du Bois:
Negro Leader in a Time of Crisis* (Stanford: Stanford University Press, 1959),
pp. 75–81; and W. E. B. Du Bois, *The Souls of Black Folk* (Greenwich, Conn.:
Fawcett Publications, Inc., 1961 reprinting), chap. 3.

and generally to act as a publication bureau for the getting of facts and statistics before the public.[10]

Though he could not then have realized it, Villard had outlined many of the functions and activities that eventually formed the working design of the NAACP, which he helped to establish one year later. Similarly, a Boston patrician and former president of the American Bar Association, Moorfield Storey, declared in March 1911 that even when Negroes became the property-holding, self-supporting community members that Booker T. Washington had so long advocated, there nevertheless existed no guarantee that black men might enjoy these advances. Indeed, Storey asserted:

The object of the National Association [for the Advancement of Colored People] is to create an organization which will endeavor to smooth the path of the Negro race upward, and create a public opinion which will frown upon discrimination against their property rights, which will endeavor to see that they get in the courts the same justice that is given to their white neighbors, and that they are not discriminated against as they are now all over the country. We want to make race prejudice if we can as unfashionable as it is now fashionable.[11]

In 1912 the NAACP's *Annual Report* announced programmatic objectives that included an assault upon lynching, disfranchisement, educational inequality, discrimination in public accommodations, and racial employment inequities.[12] These broad, basic goals

[10] Oswald Garrison Villard to Booker T. Washington, January 27, 1908, Oswald Garrison Villard Papers, Houghton Library, Harvard University (by permission of the Harvard College Library).

[11] Moorfield Storey to Ellen Mason, March 17, 1911, quoted in M. A. De-Wolfe Howe, *Portrait of an Independent: Moorfield Storey* (Boston: Houghton Mifflin Company, 1932), pp. 252–254. Storey was the NAACP's first president. See also the comments of John Haynes Holmes, one of the Association's founders, in his book, *I Speak for Myself* (New York: Harper and Bros., 1959), pp. 197–198, for a further indication of the NAACP's initial purposes.

[12] NAACP, *Annual Report for 1911* (New York, 1912); see also, Warren D. St. James, *The National Association for the Advancement of Colored People:*

were reasserted in 1915 by W. E. B. Du Bois, one of the Association's founders, when he outlined the need to "make American courts either build up a body of decisions which will protect the plain legal rights of American citizens or make them tear down the civil and political rights of all citizens in order to oppress a few." After listing the varied steps Negroes must take in their own behalf, Du Bois declared:

For the accomplishment of all these ends we must organize. Organization among us already has gone far but it must go much further and higher. Organization is sacrifice. It is sacrifice of opinions, of time, of work, and of money, but it is, after all, the cheapest way of buying the most priceless of gifts—freedom and efficiency. I thank God that most of the money that supports the National Association for the Advancement of Colored People comes from black hands; a still larger proportion must so come, and we must not only support but control this and similar organizations and hold them unwaveringly to our objects, our aims and our ideals.[13]

This was a clear call, a set of marching orders, that envisioned the "organized Negro" mobilized as one. This was the marriage of a program and an instrument for achieving redress.

From the outset, the NAACP sought to effect change by educating the public and its politicians to the need for and wisdom of reform, by lobbying for corrective legislation, by securing favorable court decisions, and by shaping a nationwide organization through which the black man, with interested white persons, could work for fundamental reforms. In so doing, the NAACP became and remained the major voice of the Negro protest movement down to the late 1950's. Though the Association was not alone in its work, it was predominant. The National Urban League, founded in 1911,

---

A Case Study in Pressure Groups (New York: Exposition Press, 1958), pp. 42–43.

[13] W. E. B. Du Bois, "The Immediate Program of the American Negro," *The Crisis*, 9 (April, 1915), 310–312.

represented another interracial, nationwide organization concerned with interracial justice, but the Urban League under Eugene Kinckle Jones and Lester Granger put its emphasis primarily upon equal employment opportunities and left to the NAACP the tasks of dealing with the public, the courts, Congress and the state legislatures, and the White House on matters of a more general and varied kind.[14] Other organizations advocated interracial reform in this century, but few achieved the status, membership, and financial resources of the NAACP.[15] A. Philip Randolph's Brotherhood of Sleeping Car Porters and Maids basically concerned itself with trade-union activities, and, indeed, the BSCP had to rely upon NAACP endorsement and support to get underway in the mid-1920's. Randolph's March on Washington Movement of the 1940's was short-lived and looked to the NAACP to press its objectives of fair employment practices legislation in the state and federal legislatures.[16] The American Communist party (CP-USA) was often outspoken and strident in its demands for Negro rights, whenever these assertions did not jeopardize its standing with the world-wide Communist movement and did not run counter to directives from Moscow. But the various organizations founded or controlled by the

[14] Personal interview, Lester Granger, July 16, 1964.

[15] On the basis of membership figures reported by the branches to the national office in New York, the NAACP had 91,203 members in 1919, 21,402 in 1929, 53,765 in 1939, 172,942 in 1949, and 302,079 in 1958 (figures supplied the author by Miss Lucille Black, NAACP Membership Secretary, in letters to the author, April 16, 1959, and July 23, 1962).

[16] Randolph's dramatic proposal for a march on Washington, D.C., in June of 1941 had forced the NAACP to open cooperation with his plans, but when it appeared that his movement might develop into a permanent organization, the Association had misgivings (Minutes of the Meeting of the Board of Directors, September 14, 1942, NAACP Files, hereafter referred to as Board Minutes). Herbert Garfinkel has explained why the March on Washington Movement did not achieve, for reasons of both internal and external dynamics, the permanent organizational status its friends and sponsors sought: *When Negroes March: The March on Washington Movement in the Organizational Politics for FEPC* (Glencoe, Ill: The Free Press, 1959).

CP-USA were limited in impact and low in membership, and were sometimes diverted from the cause of Negro rights by inner-group frictions and broader policy commitments.[17] Moreover, they often proved to be divisive forces by the manner in which they attacked the NAACP as a tool of "capitalist" interests.[18] Many of these deficiencies were evident in the conduct of the League of Struggle for Negro Rights in the late 1920's and early Depression years, the International Labor Defense of the 1930's, the National Negro Congress of the late 1930's, and the Civil Rights Congress during the Truman years.

Not until the late 1950's and the 1960's did other organizations with any broad national appeal, participation, and impact enter the public arena either to challenge or work with the NAACP. The most striking examples, of course, are Martin Luther King, Jr.'s Southern Christian Leadership Conference, founded in 1957; James Farmer's Congress of Racial Equality (originally established in 1942, but not well known nationally until the Freedom Rides of 1961), and the Student Nonviolent Coordinating Committee organized in the spring of 1960. None of these groups relied heavily on the pattern of a rationalized, institutionalized organizational structure anchored on a strong central headquarters staff and board of directors in the fashion of the NAACP.[19] Functionally, these or-

17 Wilson Record has examined the activities of the Communist party in civil rights and the variations in the party's conduct, from open condemnation to ad hoc and uneasy collaboration, toward the NAACP: *The Negro and the Communist Party* (Chapel Hill: University of North Carolina Press, 1951), and *Race and Radicalism* (Ithaca, N.Y.: Cornell University Press, 1964).

18 Grace M. Burnham to Roger Baldwin, January 20, 1930, "Board of Directors Correspondence, 1934–41," II, 28, in the American Fund for Public Service Collection, New York City Public Library; Robert Minor, "The Negro and His Judases," *The Communist*, 10 (July, 1931), 639; Cecil S. Hope, "The Flames of Lynch-Law Spread," *Labor Defender* (December, 1931), 237, in the Schomburg Collection, New York City Public Library.

19 SCLC, of course, has depended heavily on the charismatic quality of its leader, Dr. Martin Luther King, Jr., until his assassination on April 4, 1968, in Memphis, and the Reverend Ralph Abernathy, his successor; CORE had a tra-

ganizations represented a new, activist phase in the civil rights movement that employed mass participation in the tactics of direct, nonviolent protest and demonstration. The presense and performance of these three organizations reflected a disenchantment with the long-established activities of the NAACP, though, ironically, their new thrust was itself made possible by the NAACP's half-century of sustained effort.

To appreciate the singular role that the Association played in the years from 1909 to the late 1950's, and to understand more fully the extent to which the NAACP had actually set the pace for and the style of the civil rights movement until the emergence of these three newer groups, it is essential to examine more closely the tactics and philosophy that marked the Association in its early days and continued to characterize its operations throughout most of this century.

The NAACP was, in a very fundamental and integral sense, a product of the Progressive era. Its founders included W. E. B. Du Bois, Jane Addams, Ray Stannard Baker, Ida Wells Barnett, William Lloyd Garrison, John Haynes Holmes, Florence Kelley, Henry Moskowitz, Mary White Ovington, Charles Edward Russell, Lincoln Steffans, Oswald Garrison Villard, Lillian Wald, William English Walling, Stephen S. Wise, Alexander Walters, and J. Milton Waldron[20]—an interracial mix of social workers, journalists, clergymen, educators, writers, and social critics who were perfectly indicative of the spirit and concerns of a professional, educated, middle-class, and often elitist-oriented reform element of early twentieth-century America. Moreover, the tactics employed by the

---

dition of local program initiative emanating from the branches (quite unlike the NAACP pattern of national staff and Board coordination of programmatic activities); and SNCC, with its emphasis on participant involvement, disavowed a hierarchical structure.

[20] Mary White Ovington, *How the National Association for the Advancement of Colored People Began* (New York, 1914), pamphlet published by the NAACP and available at the national offices in New York City.

Association were identical with those methods used generally by the Progressives in their attempts to check the growth and conduct of industrial trusts, regulate commerce and banking, protect women and children in factories, clean up the slums, and broaden political participation.[21] The NAACP relied on investigations of incidents and patterns of discrimination, circulated its findings and recommendations through press releases to white and Negro newspapers —and later through other communications media—held rallies and working conferences that focused on specific interracial problems, lobbied for corrective legislation in the federal and state legislatures, and litigated at all levels of the judicial system—but most especially before the Supreme Court of the United States. These tactics were designed to generate and mobilize public support, to move public officials to remedial action, and to lay the bases for additional reforms over time.

Moreover, the individuals who subsequently came to direct the affairs of the Association changed very little of its operational style. University professor Joel Spingarn, his lawyer-brother Arthur Spingarn, social worker John Shillady, author-lawyer James Weldon Johnson, lawyers Charles Houston, William Hastie, and Thurgood Marshall, publicist Walter White, and journalist Roy Wilkins were not inclined—and one is tempted almost to suggest not able —to alter the Association's emphasis on legal-judicial reform as the appropriate way for bringing white men to the point of granting black men their rights and opportunities. Accordingly, the Association set about vigorously to pursue federal legislation against

[21] Wilson Record, "Negro Intellectual Leadership in the National Association for the Advancement of Colored People: 1910–1940," *Phylon,* 17 (Fourth Quarter, 1956), 378–379; and Robert L. Jack, *The History of the National Association for the Advancement of Colored People* (Boston: Meador Publishing Company, 1943), pp. 5–6. Richard Hofstadter in *The Age of Reform: From Bryan to F.D.R.* (New York: Vintage Books, 1960), pp. 131–173, has discussed the extent to which the reformers of the Progressive era came from the traditional, middle- and upper-class, college-educated elements of American society represented by journalists, clergymen, lawyers, and educators.

lynching (most intensively in the years 1920 to 1922, 1934 to 1940, and 1947 to 1950), to seek the passage of a congressional enactment against the poll tax (throughout the 1940's), to press during the Truman years for a Fair Employment Practices Act, to secure a series of executive orders on employment and on military service, and to work successfully for an impressive number of Supreme Court decisions that, on paper at least, assured the Negro equal opportunities in voting, housing, higher education, public schooling, and public accommodations.

At the same time, the Association fashioned a network of contacts and working relationships with important national figures, congressional staff personnel, journalists and columnists covering the Washington scene, and other reform-minded, liberal organizations that sometimes found their interests momentarily matching those of the NAACP. For example, in lobbying for the Dyer Antilynching Bill, especially during the early 1920's, James Weldon Johnson became a familiar figure on Capitol Hill, and the same can be said for Walter White in his sponsorship of the Costigan-Wagner and the Gavagan antilynching bills during the 1930's. Indeed, in January, 1938, Walter White's picture appeared on the cover of *Time* magazine,[22] and it was he in September of 1946 who led the delegation that convinced President Truman of the need to establish the Committee on Civil Rights.[23] Thurgood Marshall stepped to the middle of the public arena in heading the Association's Legal Defense and Educational Fund, Inc.—the INC Fund, and, with his outstanding success in *Brown* v. *Board of Education of Topeka*, he

[22] *Time*, 31 (January 24, 1938).

[23] Report of the Executive Secretary, September, 1946, and October, 1946, in the national files of the NAACP (hereafter referred to as Secretary's Report, NAACP Files). The NAACP materials were at the national offices in New York City before being transferred to the Manuscript Division of the Library of Congress in 1965. See *To Secure These Rights: The Report of the President's Committee on Civil Rights* (Washington, D.C.: U.S. Government Printing Office, 1947), pp. 151–173, for an indication of the fashion in which the Committee's recommendations paralleled the program objectives of the NAACP.

won enduring national fame and went on to hold two major federal posts before his appointment to the United States Supreme Court.[24] The Association was able to mobilize support for its particular activities: the establishment of the nationwide Writers League Against Lynching in 1933, the coordination of the National Committee Against Mob Violence in 1946, and Roy Wilkins' chairmanship of the Leadership Conference on Civil Rights in the 1960's are examples in point.[25] It was able to work effectively with a number of otherwise disparate organizations for goals of common concern. One can cite Walter White's efforts, in tandem with William Green of the American Federation of Labor, to block Senate confirmation of Judge John J. Parker of North Carolina to the United States Supreme Court in May of 1930, the NAACP's involvement in the Joint Committee on National Recovery in the early 1930's, its collaboration with organized labor against the Taft-Hartley Act, and its support of the United Nations.[26] As long as the basic ob-

[24] Marshall was appointed United States circuit judge for the Second Judicial Circuit in 1961, solicitor general of the United States in 1965, and a justice of the Supreme Court in 1967.

[25] Walter White to James Weldon Johnson, December 1, 1933, in James Weldon Johnson Collection, Yale University; Secretary's Report, December 7, 1933 (NAACP Files); Walter White to Mrs. Frances Day, May 27, 1947, in Arthur B. Spingarn Papers, Library of Congress; *New York Times*, May 18, 1966.

[26] Nathaniel P. Tillman, "Walter Francis White: A Study in Interest Group Leadership," Ph.D. dissertation, University of Wisconsin, 1961, pp. 86–89, 106 n. 71; St. James, *NAACP: A Case Study*, pp. 123–124; Edwin R. Embree, *13 Against the Odds* (New York: Viking Press, 1945), p. 90; Minutes of the NAACP Committee on Administration, May 5, 1930 (NAACP Files); Secretary's Report, October 5, 1933 (NAACP Files); August Meier, "Civil Rights Strategies for Negro Employment," in Arthur M. Ross and Herbert Hill, eds., *Employment, Race, and Poverty* (New York: Harcourt, Brace & World, Inc., 1967), p. 186; Board Minutes, February 14, 1949 (NAACP Files); Walter White, *A Man Called White* (New York: Viking Press, 1948), pp. 294–300, 333–335; Memorandum from the Secretary [Walter White] to the Board of Directors, September 7, 1948 (NAACP Files).

jective could be achieved without discrimination against the Negro, and as long as the objective conceivably would bring about fuller participation of black Americans in the total life of the nation, the Association was able, upon various occasions, to affiliate itself with a range of organizations that included the American Jewish Committee, the Society of Friends, the American Civil Liberties Union, the Federal (later National) Council of Churches, the League for Industrial Democracy, the Young Women's Christian Association, the Women's International League for Peace and Freedom, the National Urban League, the Atlanta-based Commission on Interracial Cooperation (and its successor, the Southern Regional Council), the Brotherhood of Sleeping Car Porters, the American Federation of Labor, and the Congress of Industrial Organizations, among others.[27] By the late 1950's, no one could doubt that the NAACP, as the chief spokesman for the Negro protest movement and as the main organizational instrument through which blacks and concerned whites hoped to achieve interracial reform, had come to national prominence, had developed a nationwide network of contacts and working relationships, had brought the plight of the Negro to the conscious attention of the public and its political leaders, and had laid the bases for major reforms.

Two basic difficulties remained. First, there was never any guarantee that white America was willing to accept reform and the hard, difficult realities that accompanied its implementation; and,

[27] National Public Affairs Committee of the Y.W.C.A., Bulletin No. III, December 14, 1936, in "Applications Favorably Acted Upon, Gifts and Loans," 1934–1938, IX, in the American Fund for Public Service Collection, New York City Public Library; *New York Times*, February 5, 1936; RG 46, 74th Cong., Antilynching Legislation Files, National Archives; Secretary's Report, December, 1949 (NAACP Files). The nature of the NAACP's collaboration with other organizations was further explained to the author in personal interviews with Lester Granger, July 16, 1964, and A. Philip Randolph, September 9, 1964.

second, the NAACP, as represented in its tactics and its leadership personnel, remained a product of middle- and upper-class, professional, educated, traditionally oriented America. Neither of these realities should stand as condemnation of the Association and of the excellent work it has performed. Neither should be taken as an indication that the Association was wrong—if value judgments are to be made—in employing, for over half a century, the legal-judicial tactics identified with its program goals. But both factors—the reluctance of white America to grant the Negro his rights and the somewhat elitist orientation of the organization in its national leadership—contributed to the Association's inability to penetrate to the core of the race problem in this country. The NAACP failed to touch and change in sufficient degree the racist attitudes of the dominant majority, and it failed to reach and mobilize in any enduring way the broad mass of black Americans who, because of the discriminations they have experienced, have been disproportionately part of a lower and lower-middle socioeconomic strata of the American society.

By acting through the NAACP, the "organized Negro" engaged in a venture that had to be undertaken. He prepared himself most carefully to confront the elements of power in America in a way that complied, in scrupulous fashion, with the ground rules established by the white majority itself. In seeking reform through the legislatures and the courts, the NAACP adopted America's core values and rules of conduct. The Association's credentials are established and impeccable, for it has functioned as part of the American system seeking to achieve reform within the limits of that system. In that sense, it has been revisionist and not revolutionary. If its efforts have fallen short, the burden of blame cannot rest on the shoulders of the NAACP—unless one wishes to accuse it of having too readily accepted, in good faith, the rules and values established by the dominant white majority.

On the charge of failing to make effective and sustained contact with the Negro masses, the Association is more culpable, although here again its failure can be laid to the backgrounds, strengths, and orientation of its leadership[28] and to the enormous problems it faced in coming to grips with injustice, rather than to any deliberate animus or omission on its part.

For all its initiative and achievements, then, and for all its care to conduct its campaigns in the best fashion, procedurally and substantively, of the American democratic system, the NAACP and its critics both recognized by the late 1950's that the promise of interracial reform was still most elusive. Indeed, the Association's severest critics were at the point of charging that such reform was illusive as well.

In large measure, the Association's perception and strategy rested on the belief that one brings about change by the gathering of evidence, by a rational and comprehensive presentation, by generating a public concern that will be transformed into political action, and by contacts with and discussions among key parties at the highest levels in the political and business communities. Time after time the Association was frustrated in this expectation of how organizations deal with highly placed leaders.

After some hesitation, W. E. B. Du Bois and certain of his associates at the NAACP publicly endorsed the one-time Southern

[28] Well educated, middle class, articulate, professionally oriented, and given to policy formulation at the highest levels, the NAACP leadership, black and white, could hardly have been expected to have developed a direct involvement with the black masses of the rural South and the Northern ghettos on a day-to-day basis. In discussing the jury in the Sweet case, for example, Mary White Ovington revealed her predilection for assuming that a man's income and occupation somehow assured his honesty, understanding, or sense of fair play: ". . . their occupations vouched for good caliber: three engineers, three high-skilled workmen, two business managers, a retired steamship steward, a pharmacist, a water-board employee, and a night watchman at the Sacred Heart Seminary" (*The Walls Came Tumbling Down* [New York: Harcourt, Brace and Co., 1947], p. 205).

Democrat, Woodrow Wilson, for President in 1912.[29] Following Wilson's inauguration, Oswald Garrison Villard tried to arrange a meeting with the new chief executive so that he could present the Association's appeal for the appointment of a federal Commission on Race that could serve as the first step in a concerted national attack on interracial injustice. To Villard's dismay, Wilson avoided such a meeting. When finally confronted by the publicist he refused to establish such a commission and admitted a reluctance to appoint Negroes to federal offices in the South "because that would be a social blunder of the worst kind."[30] Similarly, during the Presidential campaign of 1920, NAACP Executive Secretary James Weldon Johnson armed Republican strategists with extensive data about the oppressive conduct characterizing the American military occupation in Haiti. The Association wished thereby to embarrass the Wilson administration, and it hoped, too, that this assistance might lead to fruitful cooperation with an incoming Republican administration. Although the Haitian material did prove valuable in the Harding campaign, especially among Negro voters, the Association got very little cooperation and almost no action on problems of racial concern. The Dyer Antilynching Bill failed to pass a Republican Congress, the Liberian Loan proposal languished, federal appointments of Negroes in the South remained blocked, and the NAACP and the Negro community became increasingly restless with the GOP.[31] When Calvin Coolidge assumed the Presi-

[29] *The Crisis*, 4 (August, 1912), 180–181.

[30] Oswald Garrison Villard to Booker T. Washington, August 8, 1913, Oswald Garrison Villard Papers, Houghton Library, Harvard University (by permission of the Harvard College Library); Villard, *Fighting Years* (New York: Harcourt, Brace and Co., 1939), pp. 239–240.

[31] James Weldon Johnson, *Along This Way* (New York: Viking Press, 1933), pp. 357–360, 392; Norfolk *Journal and Guide*, December 30, 1922; *Afro-American*, April 6, 1923; Pittsburgh *Courier*, April 7, 1923; Chicago *Defender*, December 16, 1922, and December 30, 1922; and "Tentative Draft of Proposed Activities of the N.A.A.C.P.," submitted to the Board of Directors on February 5, 1923 (NAACP Files).

dency, he callously appointed as his personal secretary Bascom C. Slemp—a former Republican congressman from Virginia who had openly fought the Dyer Antilynching Bill.[32]

Constantly in search of friends in high quarters who might accede to the need for interracial reform, the NAACP sent a leading staff member to a meeting of Senator Robert La Follette's key advisors when he ran on a third-party ticket in 1924. Certain that Southern Democrats would not let their party attend to racial matters and angry over the treatment they had received at the hands of Republican administrations, NAACP leaders hoped that La Follette's Progressive party might find some opportunity to fit the Negro into its general scheme for socioeconomic and political reform. The staff member returned to the national offices to report bitterly that the Negro could hope for no help from that quarter.[33] Similarly, when the Association asked President Hoover's Commission on Law Enforcement (the Wickersham Commission) to study lawlessness against Negroes in its various forms of lynching, disfranchisement, peonage, mob violence, and discrimination in schools, places of public accommodation, and residential occupancy, it met with little success. Indeed, Walter White found a full year later that he could not even get a reply from President Hoover on the question of federal action against lynching.[34] In like fashion, the Association tried in vain to get Franklin Roosevelt's Attorney General, Homer Cummings, to add interracial mob violence to the agenda of the Justice Department's National Crime Conference in 1934. Later that same year, the Association also failed in its efforts to get the Justice Department to invoke the Lindbergh Kidnapping

[32] *Afro-American*, September 7, 1923; Secretary's Report, August 24, 1923 (NAACP Files); see also Walter White to Calvin Coolidge, August 22, 1923, which is filed with this Report.

[33] Board Minutes, July 14, 1924 (NAACP Files).

[34] NAACP press release, June 24, 1929, in "Board of Directors, Correspondence," 1934–1941, II, American Fund for Public Service Collection (New York City Public Library); Report of the Meeting of the Committee on Administration, October 20, 1930 (NAACP Files).

Law in the nationally publicized case of Claude Neal, a Negro who
had been abducted from Alabama and taken across the state line
into Florida where he was brutally tortured and murdered by a
lynch mob.[35]

On a number of occasions Walter White conferred directly with
Franklin Roosevelt on the matter of the Costigan-Wagner Antilynching Bill, and he was further able to lay his case before the
Chief Executive through correspondence and through personal conferences with Mrs. Eleanor Roosevelt.[36] Nonetheless, Franklin
Roosevelt would not risk a rupture with the Southern wing of his
party by making that particular bill a "must" piece of legislation.
At an October, 1934, press conference, Roosevelt replied to a query
on the antilynching bill by saying, "You will have to give me about
twenty-four hours because I will have to check up and see what I
did last year. I have forgotten it." The reporter reminded the President, "You endorsed it. You spoke several times, gave out interviews here after the Rolph thing in California." Unmoved, Roosevelt responded, "Just give me a chance to see what I said." The
following April, when asked in a press interview: "Care to comment on the Anti-lynching Bill?" he answered with a flat "No."[37]

In the next decade, the Association sought to cooperate with the

[35] Walter White to Edward Costigan, October 9, 1934; White to Homer Cummings, November 20, 1934; and Eleanor Roosevelt to White, November 23,
1934; all in Edward Costigan Papers, University of Colorado Library; and
NAACP, "The Lynching of Claude Neal" (New York, 1934, NAACP Files).
See also U.S. Senate, Subcommittee of the Committee on the Judiciary, *Hear-
ings* (S.24), 74th Cong., 1st Sess. (February 14, 1935), 42–52.

[36] Walter White to "My dear Chief" [Senator Edward Costigan], January
15, 1935; "Memorandum of the Interview of the Secretary of the N.A.A.C.P.
with the President at the White House, January 2, 1936, from 12:15 to 12:50
p.m." dated January 3, 1936; Walter White to Eleanor Roosevelt, April 20,
1934; all in the Edward Costigan Papers, University of Colorado Library; and
White to Eleanor Roosevelt, May 29, 1934, Robert F. Wagner Papers, George-
town University.

[37] Franklin D. Roosevelt Collection, PPF, one-page résumé of press conferences, Franklin D. Roosevelt Library, Hyde Park, New York.

Truman administration and with congressional liberals to win passage of a broadly structured civil rights package that included an antilynching bill, a proposal to void the poll tax, and a statutory fair employment practices measure.[38] Despite its close working relationships with the Truman administration and the extent to which the Negro vote had helped to elect the President in 1948,[39] the Association could make no progress in the Congress. Across the aisle, Republicans seemed reluctant to jeopardize their coalition with Southern Democrats; many of the Association's liberal and labor allies preferred merely to concentrate on FEPC to the detriment of other parts of the package;[40] some reform-minded congressmen were willing to push for selected parts of the package as long as the measures lacked enforcement powers; and the Wherry compromise on cloture proved to be the "worthless gesture" that the NAACP had prophesied.[41] In late 1948, the NAACP's Washington

[38] Minutes of the Annual Meeting of the NAACP, January 6, 1947 (NAACP Files); RG 46, 80th Cong., "S.2860" folder, and RG 233, 80th Cong., Anti-Lynching Legislation Files, National Archives.

[39] Secretary's Report, September, 1946, and October, 1946 (NAACP Files); *New York Times*, June 30, 1947; *The Crisis*, 54 (July, 1947), 200; Marian Wynn Perry, NAACP assistant special counsel, to Stephen J. Spingarn, January 20, 1948, in the S. J. Spingarn Papers, Harry S. Truman Library; Walter White to Harry S. Truman, May 1, 1950, and Truman to White, May 4, 1950, in the President's Personal File, Harry S. Truman Library; Meier and Rudwick, *From Plantation to Ghetto*, p. 219.

[40] See letters to and from Earl Michener, chairman of the House Judiciary Committee, in RG 233, 80th Cong., Anti-Lynching Legislation Files, National Archives; Secretary's Report, February, 1947, May, 1948, April, 1949, and June, 1949, and NAACP Washington Bureau Report [to the NAACP Board of Directors], June, 1947, and May 6, 1949 (all in NAACP Files). See also Special Memorandum, Leslie Perry to the NAACP National Office, December 8, 1948, in the Arthur B. Spingarn Papers, Library of Congress, for an indication of the difficulties that the Association and its measures would face in the Eighty-first Congress.

[41] Personal interviews with Brooks Hays, June 24, 1964, and Claude Pepper, September 19, 1968; Board Minutes, January 3, 1949, February 14, 1949, and March 14, 1949 (NAACP Files); Secretary's Report, April, 1949 (NAACP Files); *New York Times*, March 18, 1949; *Congressional Record*, 81st Cong.,

Bureau administrator, Leslie Perry, disconsolately reported that it was impossible to predict who might step forward to sponsor civil rights measures with any vigor, in the new Eighty-first Congress, because even the "Democrats, particularly in the Senate, have manifested only the slightest interest in introducing and working for any of these bills."[42]

Of course, instances in which Negro protest spokesmen have been disappointed in the response and in the actions of white leaders have occurred so often that there is neither opportunity nor need to catalog them further. The point remains that the "organized Negro," in working with the "organized political leader," the "organized labor leader," and the "organized liberal-reformist," repeatedly found that satisfactory personal relationships and some degree of agreement about the desirability of measures in no sense assured the passage of particular pieces of legislation or the implementation of designated program objectives. Such constant disappointments do not in themselves justify a blanket condemnation of NAACP efforts to move the power structure through lobbying and pressure-group tactics. However, it is necessary to understand that Washington—that most political of all towns—is the town of the "insider." To get "inside," to move into and function effectively within the network of political and interest-group give-and-take, it is necessary—to use a colloquialism—to play the game to the fullest. No evidence exists that the NAACP ever played the Washington game in an unsavory sense; there is no indication whatever that the Association or its spokesmen engaged in bribes or illegal intimidations, in underhanded techniques. It did function in a most straightforward and energetic fashion within the best accepted limits of the lobbying game, and so it continuously ran the risk of

1st Sess. (March 15, 1949), 2509 (March 17, 1949), 2662–2724 (March 25, 1949), 3152–3153, and (July 26, 1949), 10189.

[42] Special Memorandum, Leslie Perry to the NAACP National Office, December 8, 1948, in the Arthur B. Spingarn Papers, Library of Congress.

having to sacrifice part of its objectives in a trade-off, of having to temper its programs to achieve minimal gains, and, on occasion, of seeing its interests simply discounted by those who had more leverage. Such is the lot of the lobbyist and protest leader, but, when that lobbyist is black and speaks for an oppressed minority, his difficulties are compounded many times over. Perhaps that, after all, represents more a failing of those who run the game than it does of those who participate in good faith.

While white conservatives frequently charged it with radical, extremist, subversive intentions, the NAACP was sometimes denounced by elements in the Negro community more radical than itself. For example, in the early 1920's Marcus Garvey, black nationalist leader of his day and founder of the Universal Negro Improvement Association, asserted that Du Bois and his colleagues were worse enemies of the black people than the racist Ku Klux Klan. Interracial accommodation and rapport, Garvey declared, were meaningless and dysfunctional delusions bound to work to the black man's disadvantage.[43] In the early Depression years, and once again at the end of the 1930's, the American Communist party condemned the Association as a "tool" of capitalist interests and as "mis-leaders" who could not hope to breach the American status quo on race.[44] And, of course, in the mid-1960's black militants on a number of occasions have criticized NAACP tactics and philosophies as inoperative instruments for the confrontation with white racism.[45] In each of these instances, the "organized Negro" working

[43] Amy Jacques-Garvey, ed., *Philosophy and Opinions of Marcus Garvey* (New York: Universal Publishing House, 1925), pp. 38–39; E. David Cronon, *Black Moses* (Madison: University of Wisconsin Press, 1955), pp. 183–195.

[44] Minor, "The Negro and His Judases," p. 639; Walter White, "The Negro and the Communists," *Harper's Magazine*, 164 (December, 1931), 66–68; *Daily Worker*, February 21, 1934; personal interview with columnist Ted Poston, December 13, 1962.

[45] Many civil rights field workers in the fall of 1964 had come to discount the possibility that change in any meaningful form for the black man in America could result from efforts to work with those in positions of authority, either

through the NAACP was charged with "playing the white man's game" to the harm and detriment of black men's interests.

Moreover, there were occasions on which leading figures within the Association disagreed hotly on tactics, strategies, and objectives. However, dissidents were seldom able to win in a test with the organization's traditional, national leaders, and though certain new programs or organizational structures were discussed, and in some instances actually fashioned, the program and the top echelons of the organization seldom looked very different after the controversy than they had before. This was surely the case on the two occasions, 1934 and 1948, when W. E. B. Du Bois lost his test of strength with Walter White and the white traditionalists on the Board of Directors.[46] Similarly, efforts in the past several years to displace some of the senior Board members with Young Turks have also proved unsuccessful.[47] However much one may applaud or lament the fact, Roy Wilkins and the NAACP programs of today are the lineal

---

inside or outside the government—an important component that had always been at the heart of NAACP tactics (personal discussions with civil rights projects workers at a special workshop series, November, 1964). For an indication of the disenchantment felt by members of the black community with the concept of school integration, see Fred Hechinger, "New Mood on Schools," *New York Times*, October 4, 1967. See also Bayard Rustin, " 'Black Power' and Coalition Politics," *Commentary*, 42 (September, 1966), 35–40, for an unsympathetic discussion of this altered mood as reflected in the tactics of black militants.

[46] W. E. B. Du Bois to the Board of Directors, June 26, 1934, filed with Board Minutes of July 9, 1934 (NAACP Files); Du Bois to Abram Harris, January 16, 1934, W. E. B. Du Bois Papers, in the possession of Herbert Aptheker, New York City; W. E. B. Du Bois, *Dusk of Dawn* (New York: Harcourt, Brace & World, Inc., 1940), p. 302; Du Bois, "My Relations with the N.A.A.C.P.," a fifteen-page mimeographed typescript, 1948, Mooreland Collection, Howard University Library; Du Bois, "The Problems of Negro Organization," thirty-five-page typescript, November 17, 1948, W. E. B. Du Bois Papers, Fisk University Library.

[47] See, for example, *New York Times*, November 2, 1966, and January 4, 1967; also, Alfred Baker Lewis to the Editor, *ibid.*, April 8, 1963. When Lewis M. Steel, associate counsel of the NAACP, wrote an article critical of the Su-

descendants of Walter White, Joel Spingarn, James Weldon Johnson, Oswald Garrison Villard, and the early W. E. B. Du Bois and
of the tactics they utilized.

Perhaps the most widely acclaimed and dramatic NAACP success occurred on May 17, 1954. Critics and defenders alike of the
unanimous Supreme Court decision in *Brown* v. *Board of Education*[48] made the mistake, each in his own way, of assuming that this
victory would produce some startling change in race relations. For
the former, it seemed a clear indication that the old, familiar
America was in dire peril, and it brought forth a wide range of
reactions that included the Southern Manifesto within Congress,[49]
the emergence of White Citizen's Councils throughout the South,
concerted tactics of delay and obstruction by Southern governors
and state legislators, and a denunciation of the Warren Court by
conservatives and reactionaries throughout the country. For their
part, the NAACP and the Negro community set about to implement the high hopes of the Brown Case, and they looked forward
to celebrating the centennial of the Emancipation Proclamation in
a condition of life that might at least approach full citizenship
rights and open participation in community and national affairs.[50]
In this they were to be bitterly disappointed, and perhaps nothing
so much as the failure of *Brown* v. *Board of Education* to become a
working reality has convinced many black Americans, particularly
restless, younger militants, that the NAACP tactics have been ill-
chosen as instruments for meeting black men's needs.

For a time during the past dozen or so years, an answer to our
dilemma seemed to lie in the philosophy and practice of direct,

---

preme Court, he was fired the day after the piece appeared in the *New York
Times Magazine* (*ibid.*, October 15, 1968).

[48] 347 U.S. 483 (1954).

[49] *Congressional Record*, 84th Cong., 2nd Sess. (March 12, 1956), 4460–4461,
4515–4516.

[50] *The Crisis*, 62 (June–July, 1955), 337–340, 381.

participatory, mass, nonviolent protest. Highlighted by the Montgomery bus boycott in 1955, the Greensboro sit-in of 1960, the Freedom Rides of the following year, and the Mississippi Summer Project of 1964, and carried forward by SCLC, SNCC, and CORE, nonviolent protest became the vehicle by which all those, black or white, who chose to do so could put their bodies on the line in utilizing techniques that went beyond methods the "organized Negro" had employed in litigation and lobbying. The demonstrators rightfully claimed a large share of the credit for dramatizing racial injustices and for helping to achieve a ground swell that produced the legislative successes of the Civil Rights Acts of 1957, 1960, and 1964, and the Voting Rights Act of 1965. But two things need to be said about that ground swell: first of all, it was aided by a national revulsion for the violence employed by Southern racists in Birmingham, in Neshoba County, Mississippi, and at the Selma Bridge; and second, the courageous and imaginative conduct of the activists notwithstanding, that ground swell could not have occurred in the absence of a five-decade effort by the NAACP to test and counter the most extreme white racist patterns.

In 1964 and 1965 we enjoyed a brief moment of optimism, when it appeared as though commitments to nonviolent protests could move the nation, could effect a happy union between need and action, and could fuse a divided people into a healthy, truly democratic whole. The Twenty-fourth Amendment, the Civil Rights Act of 1964, the Economic Opportunity Act of that same summer, President Johnson's commencement address at Howard University on June 4, 1965, and the Voting Rights Act validated that optimism. But something had already happened to convince civil rights activists that it was impossible to work in good faith with the white society. The symbolic event—and we may each place varying interpretations on its substantive nature—occurred in August of 1964 with the failure of the Mississippi Freedom Democratic Party to be seated at the Democratic Party's Atlantic City convention. Militants came away from the experience certain that the dominant white majority, its leaders, and the organized elements that worked within its institutionalized network would not yield to, indeed, could not understand, the black man's sacrifices and appeals.[51] That following winter, black SNCC field workers decided they must take over the organization themselves and never again surrender its direction to white liberals; in the summer of 1966 the civil rights movement splintered on the rock of black power during the march to Jackson, Mississippi, initiated by James Meredith.[52] From that point on, the breach has grown increasingly wider, militant assertions more strident, white fears and confusions more obvious, and the nation more surely than ever has moved to a division on racial grounds.[53] Ghetto riots of 1966, 1967, and 1968 offer raw evidence of the anger, frustration, and bitterness of black America and indicate that the Negro masses no longer wish even to act as though they expect the dominant white majority to deal with them in good faith. The anxious response of that dominant majority, the *Report of the National Advisory Commission on Civil Disorders*, gathers dust on administrators' desks in Washington and seems each day to represent a muted answer by the white society speaking back to itself.[54] The presence on the Kerner Commission of two Negroes, the executive secretary of the NAACP and the Republican

[51] Pat Watters and Reese Cleghorn, "Southern Politics and the Negro Movement: Looking to the Future," *New South*, 22 (Fall, 1967), 2–36, trace this growing conviction. Disagreements over American policies in Vietnam further divided the protest movement.

[52] *New York Times*, June 21 and June 27, 1966.

[53] For a series of vigorous statements indicating the variety characterizing Black Power, see Floyd B. Barbour, ed., *The Black Power Revolt* (Boston: Extending Horizons Books, 1968).

[54] *Report of the National Advisory Commission on Civil Disorders* (Washington, D.C.: U.S. Government Printing Office, 1968). Charging that the McCone Commission withheld part of its findings on the Watts riot of 1965, the Los Angeles Area Chapter of the National Association of Social Workers undertook to make some of these findings available in print; see Audrey Rawitscher, ed., *Riots in the City: An Addendum to the McCone Commission Report* (Los Angeles: National Association of Social Workers, Los Angeles Area Chapter, 1967).

senator from the state of Massachusetts, can hardly be said to represent any basic reply to angry black Americans, who are increasingly determined to go their own way and "do their own thing."

Sixty-five years ago, W. E. B. Du Bois rallied concerned Negroes with *The Souls of Black Folk*. Most whites and many Negro accommodationists were troubled and thought the book dangerous. But at its heart lay the recognition of the desirability of interracial cooperation as long as black and white men could function with mutual respect and from positions of mutual strength. Much of Du Bois' philosophy, expressed in that book, became the basis for the work of the NAACP; his was a call to cooperation.

Today, black militants have a different author, a different prophet to whom they may turn. Like Du Bois, Frantz Fanon was a social scientist, but his analysis in the early 1960's carried a different message. In *The Wretched of the Earth*, Fanon declared:

To tell the truth, the proof of success lies in a whole social structure being changed from the bottom up. The extraordinary importance of this change is that it is willed, called for, demanded. The need for this change exists in its crude state, impetuous and compelling, in the consciousness and in the lives of the men and women who are colonized. But the possibility of this change is equally experienced in the form of a terrifying future in the consciousness of another "species" of men and women: the colonizers.

[and:]

You do not turn any society, however primitive it may be, upside down . . . if you have not decided from the very beginning, that is to say from the actual formulation of that program, to overcome all the obstacles that you will come across in so doing. The native who decides to put the program into practice, and to become its moving force, is ready for violence at all times. From birth it is clear to him that this narrow world, strewn with prohibitions, can only be called in question by absolute violence.[55]

55 Frantz Fanon, *The Wretched of the Earth* (New York: Grove Press, Inc., 1968 reprinting), pp. 35–37.

The contrast between those two writers, each distinguished, each a moving force in his own time, etches sharply the failures we have fashioned, against the expectations we too casually held. As a nation we have not responded sufficiently to the opportunities presented by the "organized Negro"; we may soon find ourselves—black and white—facing another Negro force, a black force, mobilized for and around quite different action alternatives.

Tell It Like It Was

Suggestions on Black History*

LOUIS R. HARLAN

ANYONE SPEAKING TODAY on the subject of black history must bridge not only the growing distance between the professional historian and the teacher, but also that between both of these and the nonprofessional but intensely interested black militants who want to use history as an instrument to promote group solidarity, or a more optimistic self-image, or in some cases racial revolution or nationalism. Assuming that the primary audience is the teachers, however, we shall move on to specific suggestions of ways in which Negro themes can be woven into instruction in the classroom. The all-

* Reprinted with minor modifications as published in *Social Education*, XXXIII (April 1969), 390–395.

important contribution I can make on that line as a professional historian is in the details rather than the generalities.

First, let us consider the limits of history as a social instrument. What can it do and what can it not do to reform and remake the world? While my remarks will be addressed to the young black militants who propose to remake black history, in the storefront classrooms of the ghetto, I do not want by what I say to encourage complacency on the part of the social studies teacher. His failure and that of the professional historian to give justice to the black man in the court of history have helped to bring us to the present pass.

My mixed reaction to much of the propagandistic black history of the last few years stems as much from my social values as from my role as a professional historian. I belong to the "old-fashioned integrationist" group—the liberal and radical whites and Negroes over thirty who were engaged in the struggle for a racially integrated society in the 1950's and who still believe that the open society, to which all people have access, is a worthy and attainable goal. I realize that there is a contrary view held by those disillusioned not only by recent setbacks but also by a lifetime of being black in white America, who say that integration may be a noble dream, an iridescent dream, but still a dream. They say that integration is as much a romantic and escapist fantasy as the back-to-Africa and other escapist movements in the American black past that have taken the form of separatism. I am willing to concede the possibility that all this is so. But my integrationist views rest on a set of values, which we might consider as ideals to approach as closely as we can. Black to me is beautiful, and I want American society to have this beautiful and saving element in its make-up. On the other hand, I hope that I am not a slot-machine integrationist. I would accept and even welcome such an assertion of black power and of pluralistic cultural power as would permit black people to march proudly rather than shuffle into full participation in American society. I would urge whites to show self-restraint as

Negroes experiment with their own style, even if this takes separatist forms that we can hope will be only temporary and tactical. In other words, I accept and welcome black power in most of its forms but fear the mystique, what I might call the theology, of black separatism and black cultural nationalism that often accompanies it. Black nationalism is no worse than any other nationalism, but historians who have seen the pathological effects of nationalism in the twentieth century are in no mood to encourage new cults of nationalism or separatism or "chosen people" cults anywhere in the world.

I would say to black revolutionaries who want to enlist all of black culture but particularly black history in the cause of racial revolution, you may be right but I think you are wrong to get all "hung-up" on history. Most successful revolutions have defied history, have considered the past not a glorious heritage but a record of men's sins and follies. Revolutionaries don't need a past; they build their movement on a realistic view of the present and a glowing vision of the future. Marxism, of course, is an exception. It developed in the nineteenth century under the intellectual influence of Hegelian philosophy. Marx felt somehow that to give legitimacy to his conception he had to plunge it into the moving stream of history; he had to give it inevitability by a theory of historical determinism. As a result of this entanglement with history, Marxians have experienced real "hang-ups" when objective reality has failed to fit Marxian historical models and intuitions of historical forces, as in the example of Marxist revolutions succeeding not in the mature economies of western Europe but in the peasant societies of Russia and China.

History is more than a matter of re-creating the past in a mechanical, value-free way. The historical perspective is worth something, hard to measure but significant, for policy making, because history is actually an extension of human memory and experience. But if you try to make history jump through hoops it was not made to jump through, it may bite! Particularly if it is bad history to begin with. John Hope Franklin, the country's leading Negro historian, recently criticized black revolutionaries for their accusing and ill-informed understanding of the American Negro past. Rather than see all the black leaders of the past be given a verdict of guilty for race betrayal, says Franklin, "I would suppose that it would be best that our forebears remain obscure unobserved figures, at least at peace with the world and safe from their blaspheming progeny."

Equally deplorable to historians is the tendency of many popular black historians to change the tortured odyssey of the black man along Freedom Road into a succession of sugar-coated success stories, designed to give black children a more favorable and hopeful self-concept but dangerous because they are bad history. This is what August Meier calls "cherry-tree history," the black man's answer to the Fourth of July orator's or the Thanksgiving Day preacher's idea of our American national heritage. What good will it do to trade the old stereotypes and myths for new ones? Crispus Attucks may replace Molly Pitcher, but neither one plays a significant part in our history nor I hope in our classroom teaching about it. Did Booker T. Washington really chop down the cherry tree with his little hatchet? We couldn't care less. We don't need a lot of cotton candy about success heroes of the sports and entertainment worlds, but a realistic view of why so much of the talent and drive of black Americans has been forced into these channels. We need to get our students to face the realities of the scars of bondage and the nature of life as shaped by the institutions of Southern agriculture and the Northern urban ghetto.

Let me move on, then, from what I consider bad history because it does not afford a clear, rational view of the real world to what I would consider good history if it does afford that clear view. I'll first suggest five interpretive themes in Negro or black history, and then turn to some specific examples.

The first of these themes is the persistence of white racism. When W. E. B. Du Bois declared in 1903 that "the problem of the twentieth century is the problem of the Color Line," he was certainly prophetic, but if he had looked backward, he would have seen that it was a big problem of the nineteenth century as well. We need to take a more realistic, disillusioned look at the national record, the American way of life, in race matters. It is not a pretty picture. We do not have a liberal tradition in race relations. The white nine-tenths of the United States population, North as well as South, have since the earliest days of slavery pushed the black group to the bottom of society, a bottom shared—persistently shared—by all the other nonwhite minorities in our country, the Indians, Mexican-Americans, Chinese, Japanese, and Puerto Ricans, darker than most of us and at the bottom not because of individual or group difference in ability or potential but because they are dark and because the white nine-tenths wanted things that way. What has prevailed in American society, from the eighteenth century on, has not been the glittering generalities of the Declaration of Independence, that all men are created equal, or of the Fourteenth Amendment, that there shall be no discrimination on account of color. What has prevailed, instead, has been the white-built and white-owned and white-serving institutions of repression and subordination. What we historians need to do is stop wasting our time looking for the glints and lights of hope in our national past. The National Advisory Commission on Civil Disorders set the right tone for this reinterpretation in its report. It said, "Race prejudice has shaped our history decisively; it now threatens to affect our future." It said elsewhere, "What white Americans have never fully understood—but what the Negro can never forget—is that white society is deeply implicated in the ghetto. White institutions created it, white institutions maintain it, and white society condones it." And finally it warns in its basic conclusion, "Our nation is moving toward two societies, one black, one white—separate and unequal."

So we come to the second interpretive theme, which derives from the first. Black Americans, unlike white Americans, do not have a progressive history. Here lies the ultimate difficulty in the self-glorifying black history that is all success story—that it encounters an unbridgeable credibility gap. There may have been a glorious age in Africa, but for the black man in America the glorious age is in the future. Instead of progress upward through striving, success, and victory in the classic American pattern—up from slavery—Negroes in fact have gone from one bad situation to another, from slavery to segregation, from plantation to ghetto, from cotton patch to rat-infested slum. People used to say that the mechanical cotton picker would do what Lincoln had failed to do, really free the Negro. But where did the displaced cotton-field Negro go? To Watts, or to some similar slum and social graveyard. I would urge you to consider both the ironic perspective and the interpretations of August Meier and Elliott Rudwick's survey of Negro history, *From Plantation to Ghetto*.[1] As for the present, the Riot Commission report underscores the fact that we celebrated the civil rights gains of the past decade too early. They are important steps toward a more egalitarian future, but they have been vitiated in the present by tokenism, gradualism, and persistent racialism of the white man on the street. So the hopes and rising expectations of the black man in the street turn to ashes. When Martin Luther King told us only yesterday that he had a dream, one America, freedom for all his people, this dream was simply the American dream in black guise, the dream of winning out and having the good life. But instead of coming true, it blew up in his face, killed by white racism in one way or another.

This brings us to a third interpretive theme, which follows from the first two: the theme of the recurrence of the same challenges and responses time and again in Negro history. In other words, the cyclical character of Negro history. Let me give you a couple of

[1] August Meier and Elliott Rudwick, *From Plantation to Ghetto: History of the American Negro* (New York: Hill & Wang, 1966).

illustrations. What were the big issues involving Negro soldiers in the Civil War? First, there was the question whether they were for the war, as a white man's war, then whether they would be enlisted or drafted, then whether they should be in integrated or separate units, then whether there should be equal pay and equal opportunity to become officers, then whether they would fight bravely and the whole question of Negro morale in the face of the discrimination, then panic at the end of the war about what black men with guns, who had been taught how to use them, would do when they returned to civilian life. Now, the interesting thing about these issues of the Civil War is that when we read the history of the black soldier in the Revolution there were the same issues, and also in World Wars I and II, and even the Spanish-American War and to some extent Korea and Viet Nam. There is an amazing recurrent pattern, and it comes from the persistence of white racism and the consequent lack of basic progression in the life we have forced black men to live in white America. The more it changes, the more it is the same thing. Another illustration is the various forms of Negro response to their predicament in America. At the turn of the twentieth century, faced by the lynchings, race riots, segregation and discrimination of that day, there were three main forms of Negro response: strengthening black institutions within a segregated society, the black power way of Booker T. Washington; militant protest with a goal of integration and full participation, as symbolized by Du Bois and the Niagara Movement; and emigrationism and black nationalism, as symbolized by Bishop Henry M. Turner and later by Chief Sam and Marcus Garvey. All of these have parallels today: the black power approach of Stokely Carmichael and others, conceived of as a tactical method; the civil rights movement of the 1950's and 1960's; and separatist black nationalism of the Black Muslims and also of the faction of black power militants who are creating a mystique, a theology, and a mythological history to strengthen the lines of alienation from white America.

The three themes I have stressed so far are all in the framework of social history. So let me mention only briefly, without extended discussion, two other themes that suggest a more hopeful future for black men in America. One of these is Negro cultural history, used in both the sociologists' and anthropologists' sense of a set of patterns of behavior that have evolved and become customary among a group of people, and the other definition—the history of the artistic expression of a people. These things are so closely intertwined that they cannot be separated. But my point here is that, given the persistence of white racism, the improbability of full integration of lower-class Negroes into the larger American society in the near future, it behooves us to study more closely than we have the Negro institutions built up behind the segregation wall—the family, church, business, mutual-aid, and even the low-life institutions like the numbers racket and the "pushers." On the "brighter" side of the coin, we need to study and to include in our teaching about the Negro experience in America his rich cultural contribution to America through the spirituals, jazz, the dance, and a rich Southern rural Negro folklore that has distinct African roots. The capacity of Negroes to survive and preserve a degree of sanity in this society is worth study. This brings together the static and progressive themes.

The fifth theme in a way contradicts what I said before about the static and cyclical character of Negro history. There is one big new element in the past half-century that has wrought great changes in the lives of black folk—urbanization. And the city promises great changes also for the future. For middle-class Negroes, the city has often meant a limited liberation. They could gain status usually only by exploiting the ghetto poor, and they could not enjoy this status freely in the larger American society. For lower-class Negroes, it has too often meant a new slavery, the "dark ghetto," with its rat-infested stores and homes, its social pathology. The economics of job discrimination meant that in a typical family the father couldn't support the family and so drifted away, the mother had to work at a domestic or menial job and left the children to grow up on the streets—streets teeming with crime and corruption that a cynical white police force tolerated and exploited. But Americans tend to respond to crises, and just as the emergence of the Third World, hesitating between East and West, had more to do with the civil rights movement of the 1950's and 1960's than many of us would like to admit, so the crisis of our inner cities—not just "burn, baby, burn" but the whole stinking cancer at the heart of our urbanized lives—may in the 1970's force us into a creative response.

Let us turn from these interpretive themes, which I hope will help to provide you with a clear-eyed perspective in which to view the American racial past. I come now to a few specific suggestions.

In the first place, I would urge you to begin by dealing with concepts, with what race is and isn't. There is a rich anthropological and sociological and psychological literature on this subject, but I would recommend as a clear and authoritative reference the UNESCO Statement on Race, published in book form with explanations for the layman by Ashley Montagu. There should be a well-thumbed copy in any school library.

In dealing with the West African background of the Afro-American, you should recognize right away that this is a subject about which there is deep, basic conflict among scholars, and also that it has important implications politically, in relation to black separatism, among other things. The crux of the question is that of the thickness or thinness of African cultural survivals among New World Negroes, and by implication the larger question of the strength and health of the American Negro subculture that has evolved out of the differentness of the black man's experience in America. Everyone recognizes some Africanisms in Negro speech, song, dance, and religion, but the question is, how much, and there is not agreement on whether Negro family structure, the basic social institutional unit, is influenced by the matrifocal family of West African societies or is chiefly the product of economic or social forces of either slavery or the ghetto. The best brief treatment of the scholarly controversy is in Meier and Rudwick's *From Plantation to Ghetto*.

Slavery—I cannot imagine anyone teaching American history without talking about slavery. But in the past most of the writing was from the side of or through the eyes of the master. This was partly because it was the master who made the written record, but also because of conscious or unconscious white racism. Kenneth M. Stampp, in *The Peculiar Institution*,[2] went a long way toward correcting this. It is concerned with the effect of slavery on the slave. But more recently there has been an inclination to say that his treatment of the psychological aspects was too unsophisticated, so a historian, Stanley Elkins, and a novelist, William Styron, have made what seem to me rather unsuccessful attempts to reinterpret the psychology of the slave. I am not recommending them to you. On the other hand, the comparative treatment of slavery in the United States with that of the West Indies and South America is a very active line of scholarship right now, and you could greatly enrich your teaching on the subject using Frank Tannenbaum, *Slave and Citizen: The Negro in the Americas*; Herbert S. Klein, *Slavery in the Americas: A Comparative Study of Cuba and Virginia*; the recent articles comparing slave revolts in the New World, by Eugene Genovese; and such specialized works as Gilberto Freyre, *The Masters and the Slaves*, on Brazilian slavery.[3] A further

[2] Kenneth M. Stampp, *The Peculiar Institution* (New York: Knopf, 1956).

[3] Frank Tannenbaum, *Slave and Citizen: The Negro in the Americas*, Vintage Book V-231 (New York: Random House, 1946); Herbert S. Klein, *Slavery in the Americas: A Comparative Study of Cuba and Virginia* (Chicago: University of Chicago Press, 1967); Gilberto Freyre, *The Masters and the Slaves: A Study in the Development of Brazilian Civilization*, rev. ed. (New York: Knopf, 1964).

weakness of the literature on slavery is its emphasis on the institutional and economic rather than the human and social aspects.

The experience of Negroes in the North in both pre-Civil and post-Civil War times should be presented in the illusionless way that would explain the vigorous Negro protest movement throughout the nineteenth century and also the despair that fostered emigration movements throughout the same period. I don't want this to deteriorate into a catalog of titles, but would suggest that food for a realistic look at the Northern welcome to the Negro is available in such books as Leon Litwack, *North of Slavery*; Rayford Logan, *The Negro in American Life and Thought: The Nadir, 1877–1901*; and the documentary by James McPherson, *The Negro's Civil War: How the American Negroes Felt and Acted*.[4]

Just to touch briefly on a few other specifics: Try to view Reconstruction less in the melodramatic framework of the past, and more as a noble experiment that failed because white America mistakenly thought it could give the black man freedom without equality. When you come to segregation, don't try to pretend that it did not or does not exist, in the hope that it will go away, as some textbooks seem to. You should assume that all your history students are budding young adults who need to be brought face to face with the real world. Don't be so carried away with the Jackie Robinson story or the Negro success hero of the *Up from Slavery* type that you assume they are typical and ignore the repressions of white America. Some textbooks seem to suggest that if any Negro doesn't fight his way out of the slums as a handful of sports or entertainment heroes have, then it is his own fault.

When comparing Negroes with other ethnic minorities we

[4] Leon F. Litwack, *North of Slavery* (Chicago: University of Chicago Press, 1961); Rayford W. Logan, [new title] *Betrayal of the Negro: From Rutherford B. Hayes to Woodrow Wilson* (New York: Collier, 1965); James McPherson, ed., *The Negro's Civil War: How American Negroes Felt and Acted* (New York: Pantheon, 1965).

should take heed of Chapter 9 of the Riot Commission Report, "Comparing the Immigrant and Negro Experience." In answer to the question many white Americans ask, why the Negro has been unable to escape from poverty and the ghetto like the European immigrants, the Commission points out these facts. The maturing economy offered the Negro migrant little employment for his unskilled labor as compared with the demand for such labor when the European immigrants were coming into the country. Second, in white America, racial discrimination has put a burden on the backs of black men, keeping them out of the high-reward and high-status occupations. Third, whereas political opportunities played an important part in enabling European immigrants to escape from poverty, this avenue has been almost completely closed to Negroes. In proportion to population, the Negro proportion of important political posts is extremely low—in Mayor Daley's Chicago, as much as in Boss Tweed's New York. Fourth, there were cultural factors at play, such as the strong patriarchial families of the immigrants and the fact that small businessmen had a ready-made market in the ethnic culture of the immigrants, with their language barrier, ethnic foods, and so on. Also, slavery prevented the development of a small-business tradition among Negroes as compared with immigrants. Fifth, many descendants of European immigrants ignore the time factor; they forget how long it took them to work out of poverty, whereas the Negroes have been concentrated in the cities for only two generations. And then there is the final, somewhat intangible but important factor, that the typical European immigrant possessed and was possessed by what we call "the American dream"—the promise offered by society that with hard work and perseverance a man and his family could achieve not only material well-being but status. In contrast to this open-ended society, the Negro in the urban ghetto today faces a dead end. "New methods of escape," says the Riot Commission, "must be found for the majority of today's poor."

Finally, I urge you to acquaint your students with the beauty as well as the pathology of black life in America by assigning them reading matter in which Negroes speak directly. I have in mind the autobiographies of Douglass, Washington, Du Bois, and Malcolm X, the anthologies of Negro writing by James Weldon Johnson (*American Negro Poetry: An Anthology*), Sterling Brown, Arthur Davis, and Ulysses Lee (*The Negro Caravan*), and Alain Locke (*The New Negro: An Interpretation*), and such classics of Negro writing as Du Bois, *Souls of Black Folk*, Richard Wright's *Black Boy*, and Ralph Ellison's *The Invisible Man*.[5]

To summarize what I have tried to say, on the one hand I appeal to you to give a compensatory emphasis to the role that black people have played in the American past, but on the other hand to avoid the new distortions that would come from a propagandistic use of history to promote Negro cultural nationalism and separatism. This is not to deny that an oversimplified "cherry tree" history may serve to promote Negro pride or white compassion, but such uses of history are better left to the public outside the classroom door. Both the historian and the teacher have an obligation to a broad and balanced search for truth about the past that transcends ethnic or ideological loyalties. To fulfill this function, to promote a humanistic understanding of our fellow humans, we need to take account of a black past that has villains as well as heroes, sufferings as well as successes, shades of grey as well as black and white. And, as Mary McLeod Bethune wisely pointed out, we need both the

[5] James Weldon Johnson, *American Negro Poetry: An Anthology* (New York: Harcourt, Brace and World, 1931); Sterling A. Brown, Arthur P. Davis, and Ulysses Lee, eds., *The Negro Caravan* (New York: Dryden Press, 1941); Alain Locke, ed., *The New Negro: An Interpretation* (New York: Arno Press, 1968); W. E. B. Du Bois, *Souls of Black Folk*, in John Hope Franklin, ed., *Three Negro Classics* (New York: Avon Press, 1966); Richard Wright, *Black Boy* (New York: Harper and Row, 1945); Ralph Ellison, *The Invisible Man* (New York: Random House, 1952).

white and the black keys to play the piano. The black past, in the American context, must be presented in meaningful relation to the parallel and converging experiences of white Americans. The slogan *E pluribus unum*, one out of many, may have come upon hard times recently, but it is even so the framework in which black history and all other history must be placed, unless we are going to abandon America's noblest dream.

Notes on the Contributors

HENRY A. BULLOCK is a professor of history and sociology at The University of Texas at Austin. His book *A History of Negro Education in the South: From 1619 to the Present* won the Bancroft Prize for history in 1968.

THOMAS R. CRIPPS is a professor of history at Morgan State College in Baltimore. He has completed a thirty-five–show television series on Negro life in America for the Westinghouse Broadcasting Company. He is presently completing a study of the Negro in film and has written several articles.

LOUIS R. HARLAN is a professor of history at the University of Maryland. Author of *Separate and Unequal: Public School Campaigns in the Southern Seaboard States, 1901–1915*, he is at work on a biography of Booker T. Washington and is editing Washington's papers.

WILLIAM S. McFEELY is an associate professor of history at Yale University. He has written *Yankee Stepfather: General O. O. Howard and the Freedmen* and is working on a political biography of Ulysses S. Grant.

AUGUST MEIER is a university professor of history and senior research fellow, Center for Urban Regionalism, at Kent State University. He is author of *Negro Thought in America, 1880–1915* and, in collaboration with Elliott Rudwick, is writing a history of the Congress of Racial Equality.

ELLIOTT RUDWICK is a professor of sociology and senior research fellow, Center of Urban Regionalism, at Kent State University. His published work includes *W. E. B. Du Bois: A Study in Minority Group Leadership.*

WILLIAM S. WILLIS, JR., is an associate professor of anthropology at Southern Methodist University and a research associate at the Smithsonian Institution in Washington, D.C. He is at work on a study of race relations on the Southern colonial frontier, a subject on which he has written several articles.

ROBERT ZANGRANDO is history editor of the Yale University Press and a lecturer in history at Yale University. His book on the NAACP and the antilynching campaigns from World I to the 1950's will be published in the near future. He is co-editor, with Albert P. Blaustein, of *Civil Rights and the American Negro: A Documentary History.*

ARTHUR ZILVERSMIT is an associate professor of history at Lake Forest College. He has published *The First Emancipation: The Abolition of Slavery in the North* and has taught black history since 1963.

Index